This Text Book is useful for Savitribai Phule Pune University and other Universities of Maharashtra as well as Competitive Exams.

Political Science

Administrative Theory

(POL - 502 MJ)

M.A. - I (Sem. - I)

As per New Education Policy (2020)

Dr. Jyoti Bidlan
(M.A., NET, Ph.D.)
Hind Seva Mandal's Institute Pemraj Sarda College, Ahmednagar.

2023

Price - 115/

SUCCESS PUBLICATIONS

Published by
Dr. Rajesh M. Patne
Success Publications
Radha Krishna Apartment, 535, Shaniwar Peth,
Appa Balwant Chowk, Opp. Prabhat Talkies, Pune - 411 030.
Ph. 24434662, Mobile : 9325315464.

Edition
2023

Edited By
Mr. Valmik Gaikwad

Typesetting, Layout
Mr. Valmik Gaikwad

Cover Designing
Miss. Varsha Lokhande

ISBN NO. – 978-81-19180-81-3

Preface

It is a matter of great pleasure for us to present this book to our esteemed readers. This book has been designed as standard text on 'Administrative Theory' for M. A. (Political Science) (Sem. - I).

This book comprehensively covers the entire syllabus of M. A. (Political Science) Course of Savitribai Phule Pune University effective from 2023 onwards. It has been written to meet the requirements of students of M. A. (Political Science). Some of the special features of the book are as follows:

1. *Full coverage of the revised syllabus of M. A. (Political Science).*

2. *Chapter outline at the beginning of each chapter to give a bird's eye view of the topics covered in the chapter.*

3. *Point wise explanation of each topic in the chapter.*

4. *Topics are logically arranged in numbered paragraphs exactly according to the modified syllabus.*

5. *Proposed questions at the end of each chapter.*

6. *Extensive use of diagrams, tables and various forms to give visual view of key concepts and techniques.*

7. *Conversational, lucid and simple language.*

Every effort has been made to provide the readers with most up-to-date and authentic material on the subject.

We are very grateful to our publisher Mrs. and Mr. Rajesh Patne who have rendered all possible assistance in bringing out this book. We wish to acknowledge our deep gratitude to staff who have assisted and helped us in preparing this book. We will consider our efforts amply rewarded in case the book proves useful to the students and teachers of the subject.

Suggestions of readers are welcome and shall be acknowledged with gratitude.

With best wishes.

By Authors

Syllabus

M. A. – I (Sem. - I) Political Science
Administrative Theory (POL-502 MJ)

Unit	Topic
1	**Major Approaches to Public Administration**
	a. Historical Approach b. Bureaucratic Approach c. Decision Making Approach d. Ecological Approach
2	**Theories of Public Administration**
	a. System Theory b. Rational Choice Theory c. Comparative Public Administration d. Development Administration
3	**New Trends in Public Administration**
	a. New Public Management b. Public Choice Approach c. Challenges of Liberalisation d. Challenges of Privatisation
4	**Governance**
	a. Good Governance b. Problems of Administrative Corruption c. Ombudsman d. Lok Pal, Lok Ayukta

INDEX

M. A. – I (Sem. - I) Political Science
Administrative Theory (POL-502 MJ)

UNIT 1

Major Approaches to Public Administration

Introduction:

An approach is a way of gaining access to the understanding of a subject or a discipline. It refers to a particular manner of dealing with the problem. Like other social sciences, in Public Administration too, there are various approaches which have been developed since the discipline was identified as an independent field of enquiry by Woodrow Wilson in 1887. Further, there has been a gradual evolution of the study of these approaches which chronologically can broadly be divided into three categories viz. Traditional or Classical, Human Relations Movement or Behavioral, and Modern or System. The present unit deals with the Classical approach having Scientific Management and Bureaucratic approaches as its main components.

1.1 Historical Approach:

The historical approach to public administration examines the development and evolution of administrative systems and practices over time. It seeks to understand how governments and bureaucracies have evolved, the factors that have shaped their structures and functions, and the lessons that can be learned from historical experiences. This approach provides valuable insights into the origins of modern public administration and the challenges and opportunities faced by governments in different historical contexts.

1.1.1 Meaning of Historical Approach:

The historical approach of public administration refers to a methodological and analytical framework used to study the development, evolution, and transformation of administrative systems, practices, and institutions over time. This approach focuses on understanding how governments and bureaucracies have evolved, the factors that have influenced their structures and functions, and the lessons that can be drawn from past experiences to inform present and future administrative practices. The historical approach seeks to provide insights into the origins of modern public administration, the challenges faced by governments in different historical contexts, and the ways in which administrative systems have adapted to changing social, political, and economic circumstances.

1.1.2 Features of Historical Approach:

Following are the features of historical approach to public administration include:

1) **Contextual Understanding:**
   The historical approach emphasizes the importance of understanding administrative practices within their historical context. It considers how societal, cultural, technological, and economic factors have shaped the development of administrative systems and influenced decision-making processes.
2) **Evolution of Administrative Practices:**
   This approach traces the evolution of administrative practices, from ancient civilizations and pre-modern societies to modern states and contemporary governance structures. It examines the ways in which administrative systems have responded to changing needs, challenges, and ideologies over time.
3) **Lessons from the Past:**
   By studying historical administrative experiences, scholars and practitioners can identify patterns, successes, and failures that offer valuable insights for addressing present-day challenges. These lessons can inform the design of more effective and responsive administrative practices.
4) **Influence of Ideas and Theories:**
   The historical approach explores the influence of key ideas, theories, and thinkers on the development of administrative systems. It examines how concepts like bureaucracy, meritocracy, separation of powers, and efficiency have shaped administrative practices and institutions.
5) **Impact of Political and Social Change:**
   The historical approach acknowledges the impact of political events, revolutions, social movements, and economic shifts on administrative systems. It recognizes that changes in governance often reflect broader societal transformations.
6) **Continuity and Change:**
   By studying administrative history, researchers can identify instances of continuity and change in administrative practices. This analysis helps to discern which practices have persisted over time and which have been modified or replaced in response to new challenges.

7) **Cultural and Comparative Analysis:**
   The historical approach allows for the examination of administrative practices across different cultures, regions, and historical periods. It helps to identify similarities and differences in administrative systems and the factors that contribute to their variations.
8) **Complexity and Nuance:**
   Recognizing the complexity and nuances of administrative development, the historical approach moves beyond simplistic explanations and accounts for multiple factors that have shaped administrative practices.
9) **Policy Implications:**
   By understanding historical precedents and the outcomes of past administrative decisions, policymakers can make more informed choices and avoid repeating mistakes.

1.1.3 Importance of Historical Approach:

The historical approach of public administration holds significant importance in understanding the development, evolution, and functioning of administrative systems. It provides valuable insights into the factors that have shaped governance structures, the challenges that have been confronted, and the lessons that can inform present and future administrative practices. The historical approach offers several key benefits and contributions that underscore its relevance in the field of public administration:

1) **Contextual Understanding:**
   Studying the historical development of public administration allows practitioners and scholars to gain a deep understanding of administrative practices within their historical context. This context-awareness helps in recognizing how societal, cultural, economic, and political factors have influenced the evolution of administrative systems and institutions.
2) **Lessons from the Past:**
   The historical approach enables the identification of patterns, successes, and failures in administrative practices. By examining historical cases and outcomes, policymakers and administrators can learn from past experiences, avoid repeating mistakes, and adopt effective strategies for addressing contemporary governance challenges.
3) **Institutional Memory:**
   Understanding the historical evolution of administrative systems helps to preserve and transmit institutional memory. This memory is crucial for continuity and learning within organizations, as it provides insights into past decisions, policies, and practices that can inform present-day decision-making.

4) **Adaptation to Change:**
The historical approach highlights how administrative systems have adapted to changing circumstances, technologies, and societal needs. This adaptability is essential in a rapidly changing world, where governments must continuously evolve to meet new challenges and opportunities.

5) **Evolution of Administrative Ideas and Theories:**
Studying the historical evolution of administrative ideas and theories provides insights into how concepts like bureaucracy, accountability, meritocracy, and public service have developed over time. This understanding allows for the refinement and adaptation of theoretical frameworks to suit contemporary contexts.

6) **Contextualizing Reforms:**
Policies and administrative reforms often reflect the specific challenges and conditions of their time. By understanding the historical context in which certain reforms were implemented, policymakers can assess the effectiveness of these reforms, adapt them to current conditions, and anticipate potential challenges.

7) **Diversity of Administrative Models:**
The historical approach reveals the diversity of administrative models that have emerged across different cultures, regions, and historical periods. This diversity underscores the need for context-specific solutions and challenges the notion of a one-size-fits-all approach to governance.

8) **Ethical Considerations:**
Studying the history of public administration can shed light on ethical dilemmas and challenges that have arisen in the past. By examining how ethical issues were addressed or not administrators can draw lessons for navigating similar ethical challenges in the present.

9) **Informed Decision-Making:**
Policymakers armed with historical insights are better equipped to make informed decisions. By analyzing past successes and failures, they can anticipate potential consequences, weigh alternatives, and design policies that are more likely to achieve desired outcomes.

10) **Academic Enrichment:**
For scholars and researchers, the historical approach offers a wealth of data and case studies for analysis. This approach fosters a deeper understanding of administrative systems, facilitates the development of new theories, and contributes to the advancement of knowledge in the field.

1.1.4 Limitations of Historical Approach:

While the historical approach to public administration offers valuable insights into the development and evolution of administrative systems, it also comes with certain limitations and challenges that should be acknowledged. These limitations can impact the interpretation of historical data, the relevance of historical lessons to contemporary contexts, and the generalizability of findings. Here are some of the key limitations of the historical approach of public administration:

1) **Limited Generalizability:**
   Historical contexts vary significantly across time and cultures. Lessons drawn from one historical period may not necessarily apply to another due to differences in political, social, economic, and technological conditions. As a result, generalizing historical insights to inform present-day decisions can be problematic.
2) **Selective Documentation:**
   Historical records and documents may not accurately represent the entirety of administrative practices and experiences. The information available for analysis might be incomplete, biased, or subject to manipulation, leading to an incomplete understanding of historical events.
3) **Interpretation Bias:**
   Interpreting historical data requires making subjective judgments and interpretations. Researchers may inadvertently impose their own biases and perspectives onto historical events, potentially leading to skewed conclusions.
4) **Historical Inaccuracy:**
   Historical records can be inaccurate or distorted due to errors, omissions, or intentional manipulation. Relying solely on historical sources may lead to misinterpretations of events and practices.
5) **Lack of Contextual Detail:**
   Historical records may not always provide sufficient contextual details to fully understand the nuances of administrative decisions and practices. This can limit the accuracy of interpretations and conclusions drawn from historical sources.
6) **Overlooking Social Dynamics:**
   Administrative decisions and practices are influenced by broader societal dynamics, including political power struggles, cultural norms, and social movements. Failing to account for these dynamics in historical analysis can result in a partial understanding of administrative changes.
7) **Complexity of Causality:**
   Determining the precise causes and effects of historical events and administrative changes can be complex. Multiple factors can contribute to a single outcome, making it challenging to attribute changes solely to administrative decisions.
8) **Anachronism:**
   Applying modern concepts and terminology to historical periods can lead to anachronism the projection of contemporary ideas onto the past. This can distort the understanding of historical practices and decisions.

9) **Lack of Contemporary Relevance:**
While historical insights are valuable, not all historical lessons are directly applicable to contemporary governance challenges. Administrative systems and societal contexts have evolved, rendering some historical practices obsolete or less relevant.

10) **Ignores Non-Historical Factors:**
The historical approach may overlook non-historical factors, such as psychological, cognitive, and behavioral influences, that also shape administrative decisions and practices. Relying solely on historical analysis may neglect these important aspects.

11) **Difficulties in Causality Attribution:**
Determining causality in historical analysis can be challenging, as multiple variables are often at play. It is often difficult to establish a direct cause-and-effect relationship between specific administrative practices and their outcomes.

12) **Lack of Prescriptive Guidance:**
While historical analysis provides insights into past events, it may not always offer clear prescriptive guidance for addressing contemporary challenges. Practical solutions require adapting historical lessons to fit the complexities of the present.

1.2 Bureaucratic Approach:

The classical approach to Public Administration focused on structural or institutional aspects of organization and ignored elements of human behaviour such as leadership, satisfaction, moral, motivation etc. The behavioural approach attempts to address these issues. It deals with scientific study of human behaviour in diverse environmental settings. Behavioural movement came into existence in the discipline of public administration in the late 1930s and early 1940s along with the Human Relations Movement. Both of these movements primarily deal with human element in the organization which was not given due importance previously by the classical scholars. However, the former has a bearing with the inter-personal relationships of the organizational employees while the latter deals with the inside of human being having focus on the place of his values and sense of rationality'. Behaviouralists believed in the philosophy that understanding of inside of the man is as important as inside of the organization. A comprehensive understanding of organizational working is difficult without an inside understanding of its employees. Initiated with the Human Relations Movement it was later extended and developed by Chester Barnard and Simon. This movement in this discipline gained popularity after Second World War. This approach primarily focused on the study of human behaviour in different administrative settings. It emerged as an alternative to provide realistic description of how people actually behave in the organization. It considers administrative system as a pattern of behaviour that depends on a network of human relations. It emphasizes on conducting and promoting scientific research relating to human behaviour. Various scholars adopted this approach while conducting several cross-national, cross– cultural, cross-temporal and inter-institutional studies in administrative behaviour. These studies ultimately proved significant in the development of the sub-discipline of comparative public administration.

1.2.1 Meaning of Behavioural Approach :

Behavioural approach refers to the scientific study of human beings in diverse administrative settings. The subject matter of this approach is human behaviour and it derives all conclusions there from. It tries to understand why officials and public employees act as they do. It applies various tools from behavioural science to understand human behaviour in varied administrative situations. Instead of focusing on rules and regulations; it conducts scientific study of individual and group behaviour in different cultural contexts. To this end the organizations have been viewed as a social system where interpersonal relations among the employees and their informal communication are given due weight. It is believed that understanding of internal dynamics of administration has a direct bearing with the behavioural understanding of its employees.

1.2.2 Development of Behavioural Approach :

The behavioral approach in public administration, also known as the behavioralist approach, emerged as a reaction to the limitations of traditional approaches and aimed to bring a more scientific and empirical perspective to the study of administrative behavior. While the behavioral approach is primarily associated with the field of psychology, its principles and methodologies has also been applied to public administration. In this essay, we will explore the development of the behavioral approach in public administration and its implications for understanding administrative behavior.

1) **Critique of Traditional Approaches:**

   The development of the behavioral approach in public administration was influenced by the critique of traditional approaches, such as classical management theory and bureaucratic theory. Critics argued that these approaches overlooked the human element in public administration and neglected the role of motivation, attitudes, and social dynamics in influencing administrative behavior. The behavioral approach sought to address these limitations by focusing on the study of actual human behavior in administrative settings.

2) **Human Relations Movement:**

   The human relations movement, which emerged in the 1930s, played a significant role in the development of the behavioral approach in public administration. The

Hawthorne studies conducted at the Western Electric Hawthorne Works in Chicago highlighted the impact of social factors on productivity and worker satisfaction. These studies challenged the assumptions of classical management theory and emphasized the importance of interpersonal relationships, motivation, and job satisfaction in shaping administrative behavior.

3) **Application of Social and Behavioral Sciences:**

The behavioral approach in public administration drew upon theories and concepts from social and behavioral sciences, such as psychology, sociology, and organizational behavior. Researchers applied theories of motivation, leadership, group dynamics, and organizational behavior to the study of administrative behavior. They sought to understand how individuals and groups behave in organizational settings and how various factors, such as incentives, norms, and social interactions, influence administrative decision-making and performance.

4) **Quantitative and Experimental Methods:**

The behavioral approach in public administration emphasized the use of quantitative and experimental methods to study administrative behavior. Researchers conducted surveys, experiments, and field studies to collect data on variables related to motivation, job satisfaction, leadership, and decision-making. These methods allowed for the systematic analysis and measurement of administrative behavior, enabling researchers to draw empirical conclusions and make predictions about administrative performance.

5) **Focus on Decision-Making and Organizational Behavior:**

The behavioral approach in public administration placed a strong emphasis on understanding decision-making processes and organizational behavior. Researchers sought to identify the factors that influence administrative decision-making, such as cognitive biases, group dynamics, and organizational culture. They also examined how administrative behavior is shaped by the structure, processes, and norms within organizations. This focus on decision-making and organizational behavior contributed to a better understanding of the complexities of public administration and the challenges faced by administrators.

6) **Implications for Public Administration Practice:**

The development of the behavioral approach had significant implications for public administration practice. It highlighted the importance of considering human factors, motivation, and organizational dynamics in the design and implementation of administrative policies and programs. The behavioral approach called for a more participatory and collaborative approach to decision-making, recognizing the value of employee engagement and empowerment. It also emphasized the role of leadership in fostering a positive work environment and motivating employees.

7) **Contemporary Behavioral Perspectives:**

In contemporary public administration, the behavioral approach has evolved into various perspectives and approaches. These include theories of public management, organizational behavior, and public policy analysis that draw on behavioral principles. For example, the theory of public management emphasizes the importance of understanding individual and group behavior in the context of public organizations. Organizational behavior theories focus on the study of individual and group behavior within organizations, while public policy analysis examines the factors influencing decision-making and policy implementation.

1.2.3 Salient Features of Behavioural Approach :

The behavioural approach in administrative studies has the following salient features:

1) **Analytical Approach:**

Behavioural approach is not an ideal approach as it does not believe in 'what should be' or 'what ought to be' rather it is an analytic approach and believes in 'what it is'. It conducts the analysis of human behaviour in different administrative settings. In contravention to the traditional outlook towards administrative problems and situations, this approach emerged as a 'new' way of looking at these problems or situations. It is essentially concerned with the scientific study of human behaviour. This approach does not concentrate on "how the administrative functionaries should behave" rather it merely explains "how they actually behave?" Thus it analyses the effectiveness of the behaviour of administrative functionaries operating in different administrative systems in a comparative perspective.

2) **Interdisciplinary in Character:**

This approach believes in the interrelatedness of all social sciences and aims to make public administration 'interdisciplinary'. In the discipline of public administration, it draws heavily from different social sciences especially from sociology and psychology for analyzing administrative behaviour in different contexts. This phenomenon has been explained by Simon more precisely. According to him, this approach makes considerable use of propositions drawn from other social sciences and of empirical data on administrative behaviour to test such prepositions in organizational contexts.

3) **Empirical Approach:**

This approach is centered on the human behaviour which cannot be tested in closed rooms. Thus it believes in the field testing or conducting empirical analysis of human behaviour. To this end, it utilizes various direct methods of data collection like field observation, controlled field experiments and laboratory studies. For instance, if we wish to study the behaviour of Haryana Police officials, we cannot conduct this study in laboratories; rather we shall have to go in the field to gather the relevant information about their behaviour.

4) Complicated Subject Matter:

The subject matter of this approach is very complex mainly because of two reasons. Firstly, it deals with the study of 'human behaviour' which in itself is very much complex and complicated and difficult to understand. A precise understanding of human behaviour of public functionaries operating in various administrative contexts is hard to claim. It is mainly because human behaviour is not static and thus less predictable. It changes with the change in time, place and setting. Secondly, this approach makes a heavy reliance on the concepts, tools, techniques and methods borrowed not only from the social sciences but also from physical sciences. This dimension further adds to the complexity of its subject matter.

5) Scientific in Character:

Another important characteristic of this approach is that it is scientific in nature as it lays emphasis on empiricism and drawing realistic judgments. It aims at replacing value judgments by empirically tested facts. In its scientific enquiry, it studies human behaviour in various administrative settings. To this end, it utilizes scientific methodology, standardized techniques and verifiable procedures. Besides, it utilizes mathematical models that impart a scientific status to this approach. Prof Arora states that this approach, to a great extent, is concerned with 'quantification, mathematization and formal theory construction' in the discipline of public administration. 4.6 Value Free Approach Another important feature of this approach is that it is value-neutral in character. In analyzing human behaviour scientifically, behaviouralists keep their own values away from their studies. They believe that since values can't be scientifically tested or proved so they do not start with any preconception or value as it vitiates the findings.

1.2.4 Contribution of Behavioural Approach :

Contribution of behavioural approach in administrative studies is as follows

1) Guides Scientific Investigations:

This approach has proved significant in guiding and motivating scientific investigations in the field of public administration. As an outcome scholars in public administration have attempted to utilize this approach as a main tool for conducting research on administrative behaviour of the public functionaries in a scientific way. For instance, various Indian scholars viz. Pai Panandikar, Kuldeep Mathur, Ramashray Roy, Shanti Kothari, and C.P. Bhambhari have taken initiatives in this regard.

2) **Systematic Theory Construction:**

This approach lays emphasis on conducting studies about the behaviour of the administrative systems embedded in different cultural settings. It is mainly because the study of the behaviour of two or more administrative systems rooted in the same cultural setting will not much deviate from one another. Therefore, if we conduct comparative studies of two or more administrative systems with same cultural settings, the comparisons would be of little significance to the literature of the discipline. In this way this approach plays a significant role in promoting inter-cultural or cross-cultural studies. However, in the field of comparative public administration very few such studies have been conducted more specifically by the western scholars such as Robert Presthus, and Michael Crozier.

3) **Extension of the Frontiers of the Discipline:**

This approach succeeded in adding a new dimension to the literature of public administration. It promoted the interest of the scholars of public administration to conduct more and more research on this aspect in different administrative settings and cultural contexts. In this regard it heavily relies on the subject matter, tools, and concepts liberally borrowed from other disciplines like sociology, psychology, mathematics, political science etc. Consequently, the interaction of public administration with other disciplines enhanced significantly. This led to the generation of new concepts and knowledge which apart from broadening the vision of the students and researchers of public administration also contributed in the enrichment of its subject matter. Such inclination of public administration towards other disciplines further proved more significant for the sub-discipline of comparative public administration towards making it more interesting.

4) **Development of New Orientation:**

This approach further proved significant in providing a new orientation to administrative thought. It emerged as a challenge against traditional way of looking at administrative problems. This approach "was a 'new' way of analyzing administrative situations. It resulted into change in focus of attention of the scholars of public administration towards the role of individuals, group dynamics and leadership in organization etc. Now the organization is considered as a social system. Change in focus led to understand the basic urges, needs and demands of administrative functionaries in different organizational settings. Currently, 'the findings and knowledge of behavioural studies are increasingly being used by organizational development practitioners in organizational redesigning and solving the organizational performance.'

1.2.5 Criticisms of Behavioural Approach :

Behavioural approach is generally criticized on the following grounds:

1) **Scientificism - a Hollow Claim:**

The critics argued that the behaviouralist's claim of 'scientificism' of this approach seems to be hollow. It is mainly because the human behaviour apart from complex is not quantifiable in precise terms. Thus its overall and comprehensive understanding in all respects is unexpected and unbelievable. It is mainly because the scientific study of human attitude, values, norms, perceptions and sentiments is very difficult. They cannot be measured in quantifiable terms in the absence of some well-developed yardstick. Further, comparison of behaviour of two or more administrative systems in diverse cultural settings is still more difficult.

2) **Overlooking Historical Perspective:**

This approach emphasized on the behavioural understanding of the administrative functionaries in different administrative settings and examines 'how they actually behave' in these settings but ignores the factors that lead to the emergence/ creation of these settings. It also ignores the circumstances under which these functionaries have to discharge their work. Thus this approach gives least or no importance to the circumstances and the historical perspectives that affects human behaviour and shape or reshapes it. The behaviouralists should not be oblivious of the fact that most of our present is an outcome of the past.

3) **Neglect of Values:**

This approach is further criticized for being value free. Behaviouralists declare themselves as purists and value neutrals, but they do have a set of values as it is impossible to be value neutral. This approach is stated to be of very less importance as it believed in the exclusion of values from the study of administrative phenomenon. However, 'any value free approach to public administration makes its study sterile and irrelevant to the vital issues of modern age.' Thus behavioural approach finds handicaps to explain the value laden or normative problems and issues of administrative organizations.

4) **Long Range Venture:**

This approach is further criticized on the ground that it involves long-range ventures. The main tool of data collection of this approach is the method of observation. Consistent observation of the administrative behaviour of the administrative functionaries over a long time can lead to draw results. Moreover the accuracy and objectivity of data so collected through this method is also difficult to determine, thus data in behaviouralism is not much dependable.

5) **Changes in Circumstances:**

Since change is the law of nature, so the behaviour of the administrative functionaries undergoes change with the passage of time. Consequently, an administrative functionary is more likely to react differently to the same circumstances at different points of time. But such changes are least acceptable to this approach.

1.3 Decision-Making Approach:

The decision-making approach in public administration focuses on understanding how decisions are made within government organizations and how these decisions impact the formulation and implementation of public policies. This approach emphasizes the processes, factors, and influences that shape decision-making within the public sector. Decision-making is a fundamental aspect of public administration, as it determines the allocation of resources, the design of policies, and the delivery of public services.

1.3.1 Meaning of Decision-making Approach:

The decision-making approach of public administration refers to a theoretical framework and analytical perspective that focuses on understanding how decisions are made within governmental and administrative contexts. It examines the processes, factors, influences, and theories that guide the choices made by public officials, administrators, and policymakers as they formulate and implement policies, allocate resources, and address various governance challenges.

1.3.2 Features of Decision-making Approach:

Following are the features of decision-making approach in public administration include:

1) **Process Analysis:**
   The decision-making approach involves dissecting the sequence of steps and stages that individuals and groups go through when making choices. This includes identifying problems, gathering information, evaluating alternatives, making decisions, implementing actions, and assessing outcomes. Understanding the decision-making process helps illuminate how different factors impact each stage.

2) **Factors and Influences:**
   This approach seeks to identify and analyze the multitude of factors that influence decision-making in the public sector. These factors can include political pressures, legal constraints, budgetary considerations, public opinion, organizational dynamics, stakeholder interests, and ethical considerations.

3) **Theoretical Foundations:**
   Various theoretical perspectives contribute to the decision-making approach, such as rational choice theory, bounded rationality, incrementalism, public choice theory, group decision-making theories, and policy networks theories. These theories provide frameworks for understanding the cognitive processes, motivations, and constraints that shape decision-making.

4) **Public Values and Ethics:**
   The decision-making approach acknowledges the importance of public values and ethical considerations in shaping decisions. Administrators must navigate complex

ethical dilemmas and uphold public values like transparency, accountability, equity, and social justice while making choices that affect the public interest.

5) **Political and Administrative Context:**
Decision-making in public administration is influenced by the broader political, legal, and administrative context. Political dynamics, legal mandates, and administrative procedures shape the options available to decision-makers and affect the outcomes of their choices.

6) **Group Dynamics:**
Given the collaborative nature of public administration, decision-making often involves groups of individuals with diverse perspectives and interests. Understanding how these groups interact, negotiate, and reach consensus or conflict is crucial for grasping the complexity of decision-making processes.

7) **Policy Implementation:**
The decision-making approach recognizes that the process of implementing policies is an integral part of decision-making. Decisions must be translated into actionable plans, resources must be allocated, and coordination among different agencies and stakeholders must be ensured to achieve desired policy outcomes.

8) **Feedback and Evaluation:**
Decision-making is an ongoing process that requires continuous feedback and evaluation. Assessing the outcomes of decisions allows for learning, adaptation, and the improvement of future decisions. Feedback loops are crucial for the effectiveness of administrative actions.

1.3.3 Importance of Decision-making Approach:

Here are several reasons why the decision-making approach is important in public administration:

1) **Effective Policy Formulation:**
By analyzing the decision-making process, policymakers can make informed choices when formulating policies. Understanding the factors that influence decisions helps ensure that policies are well-designed, evidence-based, and aligned with the needs and values of the public.

2) **Efficient Resource Allocation:**
Decision-making in public administration involves allocating limited resources to various programs, projects, and services. A thorough understanding of the decision-making process helps ensure that resources are allocated efficiently and effectively to achieve the best possible outcomes.

3) **Transparency and Accountability:**
Transparent decision-making processes enhance accountability and public trust. When decisions are made openly and based on clear criteria, citizens can better

understand how and why specific choices are made, leading to increased accountability of public officials.

4) **Public Participation and Engagement:**
An understanding of decision-making processes allows for greater public participation and engagement. When citizens are informed about decision-making procedures and have opportunities to provide input, policies and actions are more likely to reflect the diverse needs and preferences of the population.

5) **Ethical and Value-Based Choices:**
The decision-making approach emphasizes the role of ethics and public values in shaping decisions. This ensures that choices made by administrators and policymakers are aligned with ethical principles, public interests, and societal norms.

6) **Mitigating Bias and Inequity:**
Analyzing decision-making processes helps identify biases and inequities that may influence choices. By recognizing and addressing these biases, public administrators can strive for more equitable outcomes in policy formulation and implementation.

7) **Evidence-Based Decision-Making:**
Understanding decision-making processes allows for a greater emphasis on evidence-based decision-making. By considering relevant data and information, policymakers can make choices that are informed by empirical evidence rather than assumptions.

8) **Improved Policy Implementation:**
Effective decision-making is integral to successful policy implementation. By understanding the factors that influence implementation decisions, administrators can anticipate challenges, allocate resources appropriately, and design strategies that facilitate the smooth execution of policies.

9) **Flexibility and Adaptation:**
Analyzing past decision-making processes enables organizations to learn from successes and failures. This knowledge allows for greater flexibility and adaptability, as administrators can adjust their approaches based on lessons learned from previous decisions.

10) **Stakeholder Collaboration:**
The decision-making approach recognizes the importance of involving diverse stakeholders in the decision-making process. Collaborative decision-making ensures that the perspectives and expertise of various groups are taken into account, resulting in more informed and well-rounded choices.

11) **Enhancing Public Services:**
A well-informed decision-making approach contributes to the design and delivery of better public services. By understanding the needs of the public and considering the

implications of various options, administrators can improve the quality and accessibility of services.

12) **Accountability and Learning:**

Analyzing decision-making processes fosters accountability by providing a clear record of the reasoning behind decisions. This record allows for retrospective evaluation, learning from mistakes, and improving future decisions.

1.3.4 Limitations of Decision-making Approach:

Here are some of the key limitations of the decision-making approach in public administration:

1) **Simplification of Complex Processes:**

Decision-making processes in public administration are often complex, involving multiple actors, interests, and variables. The decision-making approach may oversimplify these processes, leading to an incomplete understanding of the intricate dynamics at play.

2) **Subjectivity and Bias:**

The decision-making approach assumes that decision-makers are rational and objective. However, cognitive biases, personal beliefs, and political motivations can influence decisions, leading to choices that deviate from rational calculations.

3) **Information and Data Limitations:**

The accuracy of decisions relies on the quality and availability of information and data. Incomplete or inaccurate data can lead to suboptimal choices, and decision-makers may need to work with limited information.

4) **Lack of Predictive Precision:**

While the decision-making approach can provide insights into how decisions were made in the past, it may not always accurately predict future decisions or outcomes. Contexts, stakeholders, and circumstances may change, rendering past patterns less relevant.

5) **Influence of External Factors:**

Decisions made within government organizations are often influenced by external factors, including political pressures, public opinion, and global events. The decision-making approach may not fully capture the extent of these external influences.

6) **Ignoring Emotional and Psychological Factors:**

The approach may downplay the role of emotions, psychological factors, and interpersonal dynamics in decision-making processes. Emotional considerations can significantly impact choices, but they are not always easily quantifiable or predictable.

7) **Lack of Contextual Nuance:**

   The decision-making approach may overlook the unique contextual factors that shape decisions in specific cases. Choices made in one situation may not be directly transferable to another due to differences in culture, history, and governance structures.

8) **Limited Scope of Decision Factors:**

   The approach may not encompass all the factors that influence decision-making in public administration. It may emphasize rational considerations while overlooking ethical, social, and cultural dimensions that are integral to the decision-making process.

9) **Inability to Capture Unconventional Approaches:**

   Certain public administration decisions may not conform to standard rational or incremental models. Innovations, disruptions, and paradigm shifts may be overlooked by the approach, limiting its applicability.

10) **Difficulty in Assessing Outcomes:**

    The decision-making approach focuses on the process of making choices, but assessing the outcomes of those choices can be complex. Outcomes may be affected by unforeseen variables, making it challenging to attribute success or failure solely to decision-making processes.

11) **Overemphasis on Formal Decision-Making:**

    The decision-making approach may focus primarily on formal decision-making processes within bureaucratic structures. Informal decision-making, informal networks and grassroots initiatives may not be adequately addressed.

12) **Limited Practical Application:**

    While the approach provides insights into decision-making processes, translating these insights into practical recommendations for improving decision-making can be challenging. The complex and context-specific nature of decision-making may hinder direct applicability.

1.4 Ecological Approach:

The ecological approach to public administration is a perspective that draws parallels between administrative systems and the ecological dynamics observed in natural ecosystems. This approach views public administration as a complex and interconnected system, influenced by various internal and external factors that interact and adapt over time. Just as ecosystems are affected by environmental changes, administrative systems are influenced by political, social, economic, and cultural forces. The ecological approach seeks to understand how these factors interact, evolve, and impact the functioning of government organizations and the delivery of public services.

1.4.1 Meaning of Ecological Approach:

The ecological approach of public administration is a theoretical framework and perspective that draws analogies between the functioning of administrative systems and the dynamics of natural ecosystems. This approach views public administration as a complex and interconnected system that interacts with its environment, adapts to changes, and maintains equilibrium to achieve effective governance and the delivery of public services. The ecological approach emphasizes the interdependence of various elements within the administrative system, as well as the impact of external factors such as political, social, economic, and cultural influences. By applying principles from ecology, this approach seeks to better understand and address the complexities and challenges faced by government organizations.

1.4.2 Features of Ecological Approach:

Here are the prominent features of the ecological approach in public administration:

1) **Interconnectedness:**

   The ecological approach emphasizes the interconnected nature of elements within a government system. Just as species in an ecosystem rely on each other for survival, different departments, agencies, and stakeholders within public administration are interconnected and influence each other's actions. Decisions and actions in one part of the system can have ripple effects throughout the entire organization.

2) **Adaptation and Evolution:**

   Similar to how species evolve and adapt to changes in their environment, administrative systems need to evolve to address new challenges and demands. The ecological approach underscores the importance of flexibility and responsiveness within government organizations to adapt their policies, procedures, and structures over time. This adaptability ensures the continued effectiveness and relevance of administrative systems.

3) **Dynamic and Changing Nature:**

   Ecological systems are dynamic and constantly changing in response to internal and external factors. Similarly, administrative systems are subject to shifts in political landscapes, economic conditions, technological advancements, and societal values. The ecological approach recognizes that administrative systems must be agile and responsive to these changes to maintain their functionality and relevance.

4) **Holistic Perspective:**

   Rather than focusing solely on isolated parts of the administrative system, the ecological approach takes a holistic view. It considers the system as a whole, recognizing that changes in one area can impact other components of the organization. This holistic perspective encourages administrators to consider the interdependencies and interactions among various parts of the system.

5) **Feedback Mechanisms:**

Just as ecological systems rely on feedback loops to maintain stability, the ecological approach in public administration acknowledges the importance of feedback mechanisms. These mechanisms allow administrators to evaluate the impact of policies and programs, enabling them to make informed decisions based on outcomes and adjust strategies as needed.

6) **Complex Interactions and Diversity:**

Ecological systems are characterized by their complexity, including diverse interactions among various species and components. Similarly, administrative systems are complex due to the diverse range of stakeholders, interests, and factors that influence decision-making. The ecological approach recognizes the need to navigate and understand these intricate interactions.

7) **Environmental Context:**

The ecological approach acknowledges the significance of the environment in which administrative systems operate. This environment includes political, social, economic, and cultural factors that shape the context in which decisions are made and policies are implemented. Understanding and adapting to this environment is essential for effective governance.

8) **Resilience and Sustainability:**

Ecological systems exhibit resilience the ability to recover from disturbances. In the context of public administration, resilience refers to an organization's capacity to adapt to shocks and challenges while maintaining its core functions and values. The ecological approach highlights the importance of building resilience and sustainable practices within government organizations.

9) **Systems Thinking:**

Central to the ecological approach is systems thinking, which involves understanding the relationships and interactions between different components of the administrative system. Rather than focusing solely on isolated parts, administrators are encouraged to consider the broader system and its interdependencies.

10) **Balance and Harmony:**

Ecological systems seek balance and harmony to thrive. Similarly, the ecological approach encourages administrators to strive for a balance between conflicting interests, values, and objectives within public administration. This balance contributes to the overall stability and effectiveness of the administrative system.

1.4.3 Importance of Ecological Approach:

Here are several reasons highlighting the importance of the ecological approach in public administration:

1) **Comprehensive Understanding:**

   The ecological approach provides a comprehensive understanding of administrative systems by considering the interconnections and interactions among various elements. This perspective helps administrators grasp the intricate relationships between departments, stakeholders, policies, and external factors that collectively shape the functioning of government organizations.

2) **Adaptation to Change:**

   In a constantly evolving world, administrative systems need to adapt to new challenges, technologies, and societal shifts. The ecological approach emphasizes the importance of adaptability and responsiveness, enabling government organizations to adjust their strategies and practices in response to changing political, economic, and social dynamics.

3) **Holistic Decision-Making:**

   By adopting a holistic view, the ecological approach promotes well-informed and balanced decision-making. Administrators can consider the broader context, potential ripple effects, and the interdependencies among various components of the administrative system before making important policy and operational choices.

4) **Resilience and Sustainability:**

   The ecological approach emphasizes the concepts of resilience and sustainability, which are crucial for the long-term effectiveness of government organizations. By building resilience, administrative systems can better withstand shocks, crises, and unforeseen challenges. Additionally, sustainability principles help ensures that policies and actions are aligned with the long-term well-being of society and the environment.

5) **Systems Thinking:**

   Applying systems thinking from the ecological approach encourages administrators to view administrative systems as interconnected wholes, rather than isolated parts. This perspective fosters better understanding of how changes in one area can impact other areas and encourages a more integrated approach to problem-solving.

6) **Addressing Complex Issues:**

   Many governance challenges are multifaceted and involve diverse stakeholders and interests. The ecological approach equips administrators with a framework to address complex issues by considering the diversity of factors and interactions that contribute to these challenges.

7) **Enhancing Collaboration:**
The interdependent nature of administrative systems highlighted by the ecological approach underscores the importance of collaboration and coordination among various stakeholders. This approach encourages administrators to work together, leveraging the strengths of different departments and agencies to achieve common goals.

8) **Responsive Public Services:**
The ecological approach contributes to the delivery of responsive and effective public services. By understanding the dynamic interactions between government and the public, administrators can tailor services to meet evolving needs and expectations.

9) **Ethical Considerations:**
The ecological approach prompts administrators to consider ethical implications and values when making decisions. This ensures that choices are aligned with principles of transparency, accountability, fairness, and social justice.

10) **Future-Proofing Government:**
By embracing the ecological approach, government organizations can better prepare for the uncertainties of the future. This approach encourages administrators to anticipate changes, plan for contingencies, and proactively address emerging challenges.

1.4.4 Importance of Ecological Approach:

Here are some of the key limitations of the ecological approach in public administration:

1) **Oversimplification:**
Applying ecological concepts to administrative systems can result in oversimplification. Administrative systems are more complex than natural ecosystems due to the involvement of human factors, political dynamics, legal structures, and cultural influences. The analogy may not fully capture the intricacies of decision-making and policy implementation.

2) **Lack of Predictive Precision:**
While ecological principles can provide insights into how administrative systems function, they may not always accurately predict future outcomes or changes. The dynamics of administrative systems are influenced by human behavior, which can be less predictable than natural ecological processes.

3) **Limited Attention to Human Factors:**
The ecological approach may not adequately address the role of human psychology, cognitive biases, and social interactions in decision-making and governance. These human factors significantly impact administrative processes but may not align directly with ecological concepts.

4) **Underestimation of Political Realities:**
Administrative systems often operate within complex political landscapes. The ecological approach may not fully capture the role of political pressures, power dynamics, and policy negotiations that shape decision-making within government organizations.

5) **Limited Emphasis on Equity and Justice:**
While the ecological approach emphasizes adaptation and balance, it may not provide sufficient guidance on addressing issues of equity, social justice, and human rights. These considerations are crucial in public administration but may not align directly with ecological principles.

6) **Overemphasis on Stability:**
Ecological systems seek stability and balance, but administrative systems often need to address disruptions, crises, and rapid changes. Relying solely on stability and balance may hinder the ability to respond effectively to urgent situations.

7) **Inadequate Attention to Legal and Regulatory Contexts:**
Administrative decisions are often guided by legal and regulatory frameworks. The ecological approach may not adequately consider the legal and institutional constraints that shape administrative actions.

8) **Incomplete Representation of Stakeholder Interests:**
While the ecological approach acknowledges interdependencies, it may not fully account for the diverse range of stakeholder interests and power dynamics that influence decision-making within administrative systems.

9) **Lack of Practical Guidelines:**
The ecological approach provides a conceptual framework, but it may lack specific guidelines for practical application. Administrators may struggle to translate ecological principles into actionable strategies for improving governance and decision-making.

10) **Limited Attention to Economic Considerations:**
Ecological principles may not fully address economic considerations, budget constraints, and resource allocation issues that are integral to public administration decision-making.

11) **Difficulty in Quantification:**
Ecological principles can often be quantified and measured in natural ecosystems, but this may be challenging when applied to administrative systems where variables are influenced by human behavior and societal dynamics.

Review Questions

Q.1) Answer the Following Questions:

1) Explain the Meaning and Features of Historical Approach of Public Administration.
2) Discuss the Importance of Historical Approach of Public Administration.
3) Explain the Meaning and Features of Bureaucratic Approach of Public Administration.
4) Discuss the Importance of Bureaucratic Approach of Public Administration.
5) Explain the Meaning and Features of Decision-Making Approach of Public Administration.
6) Discuss the Importance of Decision-Making Approach of Public Administration.
7) Explain the Meaning and Features of Ecological Approach of Public Administration.
8) Discuss the Importance of Ecological Approach of Public Administration.

Q.2) Write Short Notes on:

1) Limitations of Historical Approach.
2) Limitations of Bureaucratic Approach.
3) Limitations of Decision-Making Approach.
4) Limitations of Ecological Approach.

UNIT 2

Theories of Public Administration

Introduction:

Public Administration Theory is the amalgamation of history, organizational theory, social theory, political theory and related studies focused on the meanings, structures and functions of public service in all its forms. It often recounts major historical foundations for the study of bureaucracy as well as epistemological issues associated with public service as a profession and as an academic field. Generally speaking, there are three different common approaches to understanding public administration: Classical Public Administration Theory, New Public Management Theory, and Postmodern Public Administration Theory, offering different perspectives of how an administrator practices public administration. Important figures of study include: Max Weber, Frederick Winslow Taylor, Luther Gulick, Mary Parker Follett, Chester Barnard, Herbert A. Simon, and Dwight Waldo. Herbert Simon advanced a public administration theory that was informed by positivism. The influence of positivism today can be seen in journals such as the Journal of Public Administration Research and Theory and the Journal of Policy Analysis and Management. Notable Public Administration Theorist such as Max Weber expressed the importance of values in the development of public administration theory.

2.1 System Theory:

The Systems Theory of public administration is a conceptual framework that views public organizations as complex systems that interact with their environment to achieve specific goals. This theory draws from general systems theory, which was developed in various fields such as biology, physics, and engineering, and applies its principles to the study of public administration.

The Systems Theory of public administration doesn't have a single individual or group that can be credited as its sole introducer. Instead, it emerged as part of the broader application of general systems theory to the field of public administration during the mid-20th century. One of the key figures associated with the development of systems thinking in the context of public administration is Ludwig von Bertalanffy, an Austrian biologist and philosopher. He is known for formulating the principles of general systems theory, which influenced various disciplines, including public administration.

2.1.1 Meaning of System Theory:

The Systems Theory of public administration is a conceptual framework that views public organizations and administrative processes as complex systems that interact with their environment to achieve specific goals. It draws from the broader field of general systems theory, which originated in the natural sciences and was subsequently applied to various disciplines, including public administration.

2.1.2 Features of System Theory:

The System Theory of public administration is characterized by several key features that define its approach to understanding and analyzing public organizations and administrative processes within the broader context of their environment. Here are the prominent features of this theory:

1) **Systems Perspective:**
   The theory adopts a systems perspective, treating public organizations as complex systems composed of interconnected and interdependent parts that work together to achieve common goals.
2) **Interactions with the Environment:**
   Public organizations are viewed as open systems that interact with their external environment. These interactions involve the exchange of resources, information, and feedback between the organization and its surroundings.
3) **Inputs and Outputs:**
   The theory emphasizes the flow of inputs (such as resources, information, and demands) into the organization, which are transformed through internal processes into outputs (such as policies, services, regulations) that are sent back to the environment.
4) **Holistic Understanding:**
   The theory encourages a holistic understanding of public organizations by focusing on the relationships and interactions among various components within the organization and between the organization and its environment.

5) **Feedback Mechanisms:**

   Feedback loops play a crucial role in maintaining the equilibrium of the organization. The theory highlights the importance of receiving feedback from the environment and using it to make adjustments and adaptations within the organization.

6) **Adaptation and Flexibility:**

   Public organizations are expected to adapt to changes in their environment to remain effective and relevant. This adaptation involves adjusting internal processes, policies, and structures in response to evolving external conditions.

7) **Equilibrium and Balance:**

   Public organizations strive to achieve a balance between their internal processes and the demands of the environment. Equilibrium is sought through continuous monitoring, feedback, and adjustments.

8) **Hierarchy and Subsystems:**

   Larger organizations are often composed of smaller subsystems, each with its own functions and goals. These subsystems are nested within a hierarchical structure, and their interactions contribute to the overall functioning of the organization.

9) **Resource Allocation:**

   The theory acknowledges the importance of efficiently allocating resources, such as finances, personnel, and technology, to achieve organizational objectives and respond to environmental demands.

10) **Multiple Perspectives:**

    The theory encourages considering multiple perspectives and stakeholders when analyzing public organizations. This includes understanding the viewpoints of citizens, policymakers, employees, and interest groups.

11) **Complexity and Non-Linearity:**

    The theory recognizes the complexity of public organizations and administrative processes. It acknowledges that cause-and-effect relationships can be non-linear, and small changes can lead to significant impacts.

12) **Cross-Disciplinary Influence:**

    The System Theory of public administration is influenced by general systems theory, which has its roots in various disciplines such as biology, engineering, and sociology. This cross-disciplinary approach enriches the understanding of administrative systems.

2.1.3 Principles of System Theory:

At its core, the Systems Theory of public administration emphasizes the following principles:

1) **Interconnectedness:**
   Public organizations are seen as interconnected and interdependent systems composed of various components, such as departments, personnel, policies, and resources. These components work together to achieve common goals.
2) **Interactions with the Environment:**
   Public organizations exist within a larger external environment that includes political, social, economic, and cultural factors. They interact with this environment, receiving inputs (resources, information, demands) and producing outputs (policies, services, regulations).
3) **Feedback Mechanisms:**
   Feedback loops are crucial in systems theory. Public organizations receive feedback from their environment in the form of performance evaluations, citizen feedback, and changes in laws and regulations. This feedback informs adjustments and adaptations within the organization.
4) **Holistic Perspective:**
   The theory emphasizes the importance of understanding the organization as a whole, rather than analyzing its individual components in isolation. The behavior and effectiveness of the organization are a result of the interactions and relationships between its parts.
5) **Adaptation:**
   Public organizations must adapt to changes in their environment to ensure their continued functionality and relevance. Adaptation involves adjusting processes, policies, and structures to align with evolving external conditions.
6) **Equilibrium:**
   Organizations strive to maintain a balance between their internal processes and external demands. Equilibrium is achieved by responding to changes while still achieving organizational goals.
7) **Hierarchy and Subsystems:**
   Larger systems can be broken down into smaller subsystems, each with its own functions and goals. In public administration, these subsystems can represent different departments or units within an organization.
8) **Resource Allocation:**
   The theory recognizes the importance of efficiently allocating resources (financial, human, technological) to achieve organizational objectives.

2.1.4 Importance of System Theory:

The System Theory of public administration holds significant importance due to its comprehensive and holistic approach to understanding the complexities of public organizations and their interactions with their environment. Here are some key reasons why this theory is important:

1) **Comprehensive Analysis:**
   The theory provides a comprehensive framework for analyzing the various components, processes, and interactions within public organizations. This helps administrators and policymakers gain a deeper understanding of the organization as a whole.
2) **Environmental Context:**
   The theory emphasizes the importance of considering the external environment in which public organizations operate. This is crucial for aligning organizational goals, policies, and strategies with societal needs and changes.
3) **Adaptation to Change:**
   Public organizations must adapt to evolving social, political, economic, and technological conditions. The theory's focus on adaptation helps organizations stay relevant, responsive, and effective in a dynamic environment.
4) **Efficient Resource Allocation:**
   By considering the flow of inputs and outputs within the organization, the theory aids in efficient resource allocation. It helps administrators allocate resources strategically to achieve desired outcomes.
5) **Feedback and Improvement:**
   The theory encourages the establishment of feedback mechanisms, enabling organizations to receive information about their performance and make necessary improvements. This iterative process enhances the organization's effectiveness.
6) **Interdisciplinary Approach:**
   The theory draws from general systems theory and multiple disciplines, promoting a cross-disciplinary approach to public administration. This allows for a broader perspective and innovative problem-solving.
7) **Holistic Decision-Making:**
   By viewing organizations as interconnected systems, the theory encourages decision-makers to consider the potential consequences and impacts of their decisions on various aspects of the organization.
8) **Coordination and Collaboration:**
   The theory highlights the importance of coordination and collaboration among different departments and subsystems within an organization. This can lead to improved efficiency and effectiveness.
9) **Strategic Planning:**
   Organizations can use the theory to develop strategic plans that align with their goals, values, and the external environment. This helps create a clear roadmap for achieving desired outcomes.

10) Improved Performance:

Applying systems thinking can lead to improved overall organizational performance. By understanding how different parts of the organization interact, administrators can identify areas of improvement and implement targeted changes.

11) Public Service Delivery:

Effective application of the theory can lead to improved public service delivery. By optimizing internal processes and resource allocation, organizations can provide better services to citizens.

12) Policy Formulation:

The theory's focus on understanding the interplay between different elements can lead to more informed and effective policy formulation. Policies can be designed to address complex issues from a systemic perspective.

2.1.5 Limitations of System Theory:

Here are some of the key limitations of this theory:

1) Simplification:

The theory's focus on the interrelationships and interactions within organizations can sometimes oversimplify the intricate realities of administrative processes and the external environment.

2) Complexity Management:

In highly complex and dynamic environments, the theory might struggle to provide practical guidance on how to manage and balance the various interacting components effectively.

3) Difficulty in Measurement:

Some of the concepts, such as equilibrium and adaptation, are difficult to measure quantitatively, making it challenging to assess the extent to which an organization is achieving these goals.

4) Static vs. Dynamic:

The theory might not fully capture the dynamic and evolving nature of organizations and their environments. It can sometimes portray organizations as more static than they actually are.

5) Lack of Prescriptive Guidance:

The theory provides a framework for understanding systems but may lack specific prescriptive guidance on how to address certain organizational challenges or improve performance.

6) Overemphasis on Internal Processes:

While the theory emphasizes the internal interactions of an organization, it might underemphasize the influence of external factors, such as political pressures, cultural influences, and economic conditions.

7) **Resource Constraints:**
Implementing the theory's recommendations for adaptation and flexibility might be constrained by limited resources, bureaucratic barriers, and legal constraints.

8) **Limited Attention to Human Behavior:**
The theory may not fully account for the role of human behavior, motivation, and decision-making within organizations, which are critical factors in administrative processes.

9) **Ambiguity in Boundaries:**
Defining the boundaries of a system can be challenging, and this ambiguity can impact the accuracy of analysis and decision-making.

10) **Overemphasis on Rationality:**
The theory assumes a rational decision-making process, which might not always reflect the actual decision-making complexities and behavioral biases present in organizations.

11) **Cultural and Contextual Differences:**
The theory might not sufficiently account for cultural and contextual variations that can significantly impact the functioning of public organizations across different regions and contexts.

12) **Limited Practical Application:**
While the theory provides a conceptual framework, applying its principles in real-world scenarios can be challenging, as it requires adapting the theory to the specific context and circumstances of each organization.

2.2 Rational Choice Theory:

Rational choice theory, also called rational action theory **or** choice theory, school of thought based on the assumption that individuals choose a course of action that is most in line with their personal preferences. Rational choice theory is used to model human decision making, especially in the context of microeconomics, where it helps economists better understand the behaviour of a society in terms of individual actions as explained through rationality, in which choices are consistent because they are made according to personal preference. Rational choice theory increasingly is applied to other areas as well, including evolutionary theory, political science, and warfare.

2.2.1 Meaning of Rational Choice Theory:

Rational choice theory is a theory in social science that argues human behavior, and social life in general, can be explained in terms of rational choices of individuals. Social interaction, including political interaction, is considered to be a type of exchange where individuals will interact with each other if the expected gains outweigh the expected costs arising from the interaction. For example, you may decide to enter into a friendship if you believe you will get more out of the friendship than the burden the friendship will impose upon you.

2.2.2 Elements of Rational Choice Theory:

Rational Choice Theory (RCT) is a widely used theoretical framework in public administration and other social sciences. It posits that individuals and organizations make decisions based on rational calculations aimed at maximizing their self-interest or achieving specific goals. In the context of public administration, RCT examines how government agencies, officials, and citizens make decisions within a framework of constrained resources and competing objectives. The key elements of Rational Choice Theory in the context of public administration include:

1) **Individual Rationality:**
   Rational Choice Theory assumes that individuals and organizations are rational actors who make decisions based on their self-interest and a careful assessment of the available options. Rationality in this context means making choices that maximize perceived benefits and minimize costs.

2) **Goal-Oriented Behavior:**
   RCT suggests that actors in public administration have clear objectives or goals and seek to achieve these goals through their decisions and actions. Goals could include policy objectives, maximizing budget efficiency, or enhancing personal reputation.

3) **Preferences and Utilities:**
   Rational actors have well-defined preferences for outcomes and assign utilities (values) to different outcomes based on their preferences. These utilities guide decision-making by indicating which option is more favorable.

4) **Cost-Benefit Analysis:**
   RCT involves evaluating the costs and benefits associated with each available option before making a decision. Rational actors choose the option that provides the greatest net benefit (i.e., benefits minus costs).

5) **Constraints:**
   Rational actors operate within constraints, including limited resources (such as time, budget, and personnel) and institutional rules and regulations. These constraints influence decision-making and shape the range of feasible choices.

6) **Expected Utility:**
   Rational Choice Theory introduces the concept of expected utility, which involves assessing the probabilities of different outcomes and calculating the expected benefits for each option. Rational actors choose the option with the highest expected utility.

7) **Trade-offs and Compromises:**
Rational actors acknowledge that achieving certain goals might require trade-offs or compromises due to limited resources and conflicting objectives.

8) **Collective Decision-Making:**
The theory can be applied to group decision-making within public organizations. It examines how various stakeholders collectively make choices, considering divergent preferences and negotiating outcomes.

9) **Policy Analysis:**
Rational Choice Theory is often used to analyze public policy decisions. Policymakers weigh the costs and benefits of different policy options to select the one that aligns with their objectives and has the highest expected utility.

10) **Public Choice Theory:**
A subfield of Rational Choice Theory, Public Choice Theory, specifically focuses on the behavior of public officials and the influence of political factors on decision-making in government.

11) **Game Theory:**
Rational Choice Theory can also be used in conjunction with game theory, which studies strategic interactions between multiple decision-makers. Game theory helps analyze situations where the outcomes of one actor's choices depend on the choices of others.

12) **Assumptions and Critiques:**
It's important to note that Rational Choice Theory assumes perfect information, consistent preferences, and logical decision-making, which may not always reflect real-world complexities, cognitive limitations, and biases.

2.2.3 Importance of Rational Choice Theory:

Importance of rational choice theory explained with following points:

1) **Predictive Power:**
RCT's predictive capacity is invaluable in forecasting decision-making outcomes. By focusing on rational calculations, the theory enables analysts to anticipate how individuals and organizations are likely to respond to different incentives, constraints, and opportunities.

2) **Efficient Resource Allocation:**
One of RCT's fundamental principles is cost-benefit analysis. This aids public administrators in resource allocation decisions, ensuring that resources are allocated optimally to achieve desired outcomes, thereby enhancing efficiency and effectiveness.

3) **Policy Analysis:**
Rational Choice Theory proves particularly useful in policy analysis. By evaluating options based on expected utility and conducting a systematic assessment of costs and benefits, policymakers can make informed choices that align with policy goals and objectives.

4) **Incentive Design:**
The theory's insights into human responses to incentives are essential for designing effective incentive structures. Understanding how individuals react to different incentives helps design reward systems that encourage desired behaviors among public officials and employees.

5) **Understanding Bureaucratic Behavior:**
Rational Choice Theory illuminates the decision-making processes of bureaucrats. By considering the self-interest of individual bureaucrats within the confines of institutional rules, administrators gain insights into how public officials navigate their responsibilities and constraints.

6) **Strategic Decision-Making:**
RCT's focus on utility maximization and rational calculations lends itself to strategic decision-making. Public administrators can strategically align actions and choices with organizational goals, enhancing overall effectiveness and impact.

7) **Public Service Provision:**
Rational Choice Theory provides a lens to analyze how public organizations provide services to citizens. By evaluating costs, benefits, and utility, administrators can streamline service delivery and improve public satisfaction.

8) **Accountability and Transparency:**
Applying RCT to accountability mechanisms ensures that they align with rational decision-making processes. Transparent decision-making enhances accountability and builds public trust in government actions.

9) **Comparative Analysis:**
The theory facilitates comparative analyses of decision-making across different public organizations and contexts. By identifying common patterns and variations, policymakers gain insights into effective strategies and areas for improvement.

10) **Public Choice Theory:**
An extension of RCT, Public Choice Theory examines how political factors influence public decisions. It offers valuable insights into the behavior of voters, politicians, and interest groups within democratic systems, fostering a deeper understanding of political dynamics.

2.2.4 Limitations of Rational Choice Theory:

Limitations of rational choice theory explained with following points:

1) **Individual Rationality:**

At the heart of Rational Choice Theory is the assumption that individuals are rational actors who make choices based on careful consideration of available options. In the context of public administration, this means that public officials and decision-makers are motivated to make choices that best serve their self-interest, whether that involves achieving policy objectives, gaining personal recognition, or maximizing budgetary efficiency.

2) **Utility Maximization:**

Rational actors seek to maximize their utility, which represents the perceived benefit or value derived from different outcomes. In public administration, this utility can encompass a wide range of factors, from monetary gains to the enhancement of one's reputation or political standing. Decision-makers weigh the potential benefits of each choice against its associated costs.

3) **Cost-Benefit Analysis:**

Decision-making within Rational Choice Theory involves a systematic evaluation of the costs and benefits associated with various options. Public officials assess the potential gains and losses resulting from different choices, aiming to select the option that provides the highest net benefit. This approach ensures efficient resource allocation and decision-making that aligns with organizational objectives.

4) **Preferences and Orderings:**

Individuals possess distinct preferences for various outcomes. These preferences are often ranked in order of importance, guiding decision-making. In public administration, preferences can include policy priorities, budget allocations, and strategies for achieving specific goals. Rational actors choose options that align with their most preferred outcomes.

5) **Expected Utility:**

Rational Choice Theory introduces the concept of expected utility, where decision-makers assess the probabilities of different outcomes and calculate the expected benefits for each option. By evaluating the potential utility of each choice, individuals select the option with the highest expected utility, enabling informed decision-making.

6) **Constraints:**

Rational choices are made within the constraints of limited resources, time, and institutional rules. Public administrators and officials must navigate these constraints when making decisions. Budget limitations, legal regulations, and bureaucratic procedures influence the range of feasible choices available to decision-makers.

7) **Consistency and Transitivity:**

Rational Choice Theory assumes that individuals exhibit consistent preferences and transitive choices. This means that if an individual prefers option A over option B and option B over option C, then they also prefer option A over option C. This principle ensures logical and predictable decision-making behavior.

8) **Incentives:**

Rational Choice Theory recognizes the role of incentives in shaping decision-making. Public officials respond to incentives by adjusting their behavior to maximize rewards and minimize penalties. Incentives can range from performance bonuses for achieving targets to electoral support gained through policy success.

9) **Public Goods and Collective Action:**

RCT helps explain challenges related to public goods provision and collective action. Public goods, such as clean air or national security, benefit society as a whole, but individuals may hesitate to contribute to their provision if they anticipate that others will bear the cost. Rational actors weigh their contributions against the benefits received and evaluate whether their individual efforts will make a meaningful impact.

10) **Bureaucratic Behavior:**

Applying Rational Choice Theory to public administration allows for insights into bureaucratic behavior. Public officials and employees, constrained by institutional rules and policies, make choices that align with their self-interest while also fulfilling their organizational roles. The theory sheds light on how officials navigate their responsibilities, personal goals, and the expectations of their superiors.

2.3 Comparative Public Administration:

Comparative public administration focuses on Public Administration as a field of study and research rather simple execution of tasks. Haroon A. Khan defined the Comparative Public administration as a quest for searching patterns and regularities in administrative behavior and action and to characterize them in present day nation states. It is interesting to note why and how Public Administration has gained a place in the field of study. Woodrow Wilson is credited for his writing The Study of Administration and perhaps this was a starting point in the United States, in other countries like India, Germany Public Administration was known long back owing to influences of Arthashashtra and Kameralwissenschaft. Later half of twentieth century saw many improvements and bureaucratic internationalization between European countries in reference to Euro-zone and also to all other countries of the world with transnational organizations like World Bank, Interpol and International Court of Justice.

2.3.1 Meaning of Comparative Public Administration:

The Comparative Administration Group of the American Society for Public Administration which was set up in 1963 under the chairmanship of Fred Riggs to study the administrative problems of developing countries viewed in the systematic context of their social, cultural, po-litical and economic environments has defined Comparative Public Administration as "the theory of public administration applied to diverse cultures and national setting and the body of factual data, by which it can be examined and tested." Fred W. Riggs Chairman of the Administrative Comparative Group (CAG) in 1967 holds that the term 'comparative' should be used only for empirical, nomothetic studies.

2.3.2 Nature of Comparative Public Administration:

The nature of Comparative Public Administration (CPA) is rooted in the study and analysis of administrative systems, processes, and practices across different countries and contexts. It involves examining similarities, differences, patterns, and trends in public administration to gain insights into how different governments and organizations manage public affairs. CPA goes beyond the examination of a single administrative system and seeks to draw comparisons and lessons from diverse global experiences. Here are key aspects that characterize the nature of Comparative Public Administration:

1) **Cross-Country Comparison:**
   CPA involves comparing administrative practices, structures, policies, and outcomes across different countries. It allows for the identification of commonalities and variations in administrative approaches.
2) **Global Perspective:**
   The nature of CPA is global in scope. It encompasses a wide range of countries, from developed to developing, to provide a comprehensive understanding of administrative systems across different levels of economic, political, and social development.
3) **Diverse Contexts:**
   CPA takes into account the cultural, historical, political, economic, and social contexts in which public administration operates. Different contexts shape administrative practices and outcomes, influencing the way governments address challenges and deliver public services.
4) **Analytical Frameworks:**
   Researchers use various analytical frameworks to compare administrative systems. These frameworks may include structural-functional, institutional, historical, and political-cultural perspectives to analyze similarities and differences.
5) **Learning and Adaptation:**
   CPA aims to facilitate learning from the experiences of other countries. Governments can adopt successful practices and strategies while avoiding pitfalls that other countries have faced, promoting administrative innovation and improvement.

6) **Policy Transfer:**

Comparative studies allow for the transfer of policies and practices that have proven effective in one country to another, leading to policy innovation and enhancing governance.

7) **Institutional Arrangements:**

CPA explores the organizational structures, roles of public institutions, and relationships between various branches of government. Comparative analysis provides insights into how these elements influence administrative effectiveness.

8) **Development of Universal Theories:**

By comparing administrative systems, researchers can identify principles and theories that are applicable across different contexts, contributing to the development of universal theories of public administration.

9) **Challenges and Solutions:**

CPA identifies challenges faced by different countries and the strategies they employ to address these challenges. This helps policymakers understand different approaches to common problems.

10) **Diversity of Administrative Practices:**

The nature of CPA reveals the wide range of administrative practices, from bureaucratic to participatory, centralized to decentralized, hierarchical to network-based, providing a comprehensive view of administrative diversity.

11) **Accounting for Culture and Context:**

CPA recognizes that administrative practices are influenced by cultural norms, values, and historical legacies. This acknowledgment adds depth to the analysis of administrative systems.

12) **Methodological Challenges:**

Conducting comparative studies presents methodological challenges, including the need for standardized data collection, addressing linguistic and cultural biases, and ensuring the relevance of findings to specific contexts.

2.3.3 Scope of Comparative Public Administration:

The scope of CPA includes the following key dimensions:

1) **Administrative Structures and Organizations:**

CPA examines the structures, hierarchies, and organizational arrangements within different administrative systems. It investigates the roles of various government agencies, departments, and ministries, comparing how they are designed and function across countries.

2) **Bureaucratic Culture and Behavior:**

   The field explores the cultural norms, values, and behavioral patterns that shape bureaucratic behavior in various contexts. It assesses the impact of cultural factors on decision-making, accountability, and efficiency.

3) **Policy Formulation and Implementation:**

   Comparative studies in CPA focus on how policies are formulated, implemented, and evaluated across different countries. This includes analyzing the role of political institutions, administrative processes, and stakeholder involvement in policy cycles.

4) **Public Service Delivery:**

   CPA evaluates how public services are delivered to citizens, including aspects such as service quality, accessibility, and responsiveness. It examines the effectiveness of different mechanisms, such as public-private partnerships or decentralized service provision.

5) **Governance and Accountability:**

   The field assesses governance mechanisms, including the separation of powers, checks and balances, and mechanisms for holding public officials accountable. Comparative analysis sheds light on effective ways to ensure transparency and prevent corruption.

6) **Decentralization and Local Governance:**

   CPA explores the degree of decentralization and local governance structures in different countries. It examines how local governments interact with central authorities, manage resources, and address community needs.

7) **Administrative Reforms:**

   Comparative studies in CPA analyze administrative reform efforts across countries. This includes examining the motivations, strategies, and outcomes of reforms aimed at improving administrative efficiency and effectiveness.

8) **E-Government and Technological Innovation:**

   CPA investigates how countries utilize technology to enhance administrative processes and service delivery. It assesses the adoption of e-government initiatives, digital platforms, and data-driven decision-making.

9) **Policy Transfer and Lessons Learned:**

   One of the core objectives of CPA is to facilitate the transfer of successful policies and practices from one country to another. This helps governments learn from the experiences of others and adopt effective strategies.

10) **Public Administration Education and Training:**

    Comparative analysis of public administration education and training programs helps identify best practices in preparing future public servants and administrators.

11) Crisis Management and Disaster Response:

CPA explores how different administrative systems handle crises, emergencies, and natural disasters. It examines the effectiveness of disaster preparedness, response strategies, and coordination mechanisms.

12) Public Financial Management:

The field evaluates how countries manage public finances, including budgeting, taxation, public debt, and fiscal policies. Comparative analysis sheds light on effective financial management practices.

2.3.4 Importance of Comparative Public Administration:

Here are ten key reasons highlighting the importance of Comparative Public Administration:

1) Learning from Best Practices:

CPA allows governments to identify successful administrative practices from other countries and adapt them to their own context. This learning process promotes administrative innovation and efficiency improvements.

2) Policy Transfer:

Comparative studies facilitate the transfer of policies that have proven effective in one country to another. This accelerates the adoption of successful policies and strategies, saving time and resources in policy development.

3) Policy Innovation:

By examining various approaches to similar challenges, CPA encourages the generation of innovative policy ideas. Governments can draw inspiration from diverse practices to develop context-specific solutions.

4) Avoiding Pitfalls:

Learning from the mistakes and failures of other countries helps governments avoid repeating costly errors. CPA provides insights into challenges faced by other administrations and the lessons learned from addressing them.

5) Evidence-Based Decision-Making:

Comparative research in public administration is grounded in empirical evidence. Policymakers can make informed decisions by drawing on data and analyses of similar situations in other countries.

6) Enhanced Accountability:

CPA sheds light on accountability mechanisms that have proven effective in different contexts. This allows governments to design and implement accountability frameworks that ensure transparency and prevent corruption.

7) **Effective Governance Strategies:**
Through CPA, governments can identify effective governance strategies that promote citizen engagement, participation, and collaboration. This enhances the legitimacy of public policies and decisions.

8) **Cultural Sensitivity:**
Comparative studies take into account cultural and contextual factors that influence administrative practices. This approach helps governments design policies that respect cultural norms and values.

9) **Academic Advancement:**
For scholars and researchers, CPA contributes to the development of theories and models that transcend national boundaries. It advances the academic field of public administration by offering broader perspectives and insights.

10) **Global Collaboration:**
CPA fosters collaboration and knowledge sharing among countries. It provides a platform for governments to exchange experiences, share lessons, and collaborate on joint initiatives to address global challenges.

11) **Promoting International Development:**
Comparative research helps identify effective strategies for governance and public service delivery, which can be valuable for international development organizations working to improve governance in developing countries.

12) **Informing Diplomacy and International Relations:**
Comparative insights can inform diplomatic efforts by highlighting areas of convergence and divergence in administrative practices. This understanding can facilitate international cooperation and negotiations.

2.4 Development Administration:

Concept of development is not new but still it is in an incipient stage. Since civilization it has been growing in scope and substance, and the present nature of development greatly differs from that of the early period. Serious attempts have been made by scholars of different disciplines particularly after the Second World War to define the concept of development. Brandt Commission report stated that Development could never be defined to universal satisfaction. In the same note, Up off and Ilchman 1972 pointed that Development was in all probability one of the most depreciated terms in social science, literature and has been used more it has been understood. Many have defined it in terms of increase in national economy other defined it to include social improvement and still others in terms of increase in the capacity of the political system, and while there are others who make no distinction between development and modernization, development is a complex phenomenon comprising many dimensions social, political ,economic, administrative and so on Now there is trend to call as 'economic development', 'political development', 'social development', and soon. In the context of public administration, development is development administration and 'administrative development'. Then economic, political, social and administrative may be viewed as emerging from development without being development. So, while defining the concept of development, it is 20 necessary to take an integrated approach. The overall goal of development is therefore to increase the economic, political, and civil rights of all people across gender, ethnic groups, religions, races, regions and countries.

2.4.1 Meaning:

Development Administration is about projects, programs, policies and ideas which are focused at development of a nation, with the point of view of socio-economic and socio-political development of society in general, carried out by talented and skilled bureaucrats. The concept of 'development administration' has been almost exclusively used with reference to the developing nations of Asia, the Middle East, Africa and Latin America. Perhaps it was first used by Donald C. Stone, although the term was popularised by Riggs and Weidner in the 1960s. Whatever its point of origin, the conceptual genre of development administration has been distinctively Western. Two interconnected Euro-American traditions converge in it. One of these streams of administrative thought is the result of an evolving trend of scientific management that began at the turn of the century with the administrative reform movement.

2.4.2 Definitions:

Definitions of Development Administration by different scholar are as follows:

1) Harry J. Friedman:

"*Development administration means (a) Programme implementation for socio economic progress and monitoring of nation building progress and (b) Administrative reforms to keep the bureaucracy updated.*"

2) Hahn Been lee:

"*Development administration involved management of government or of an agency to ensure capability to cop up with social change and sustained growth.*"

3) Gant

"*He observed that development administration is "that aspect of Public Administration in which focus of attention is on organizing and administering public agencies in such a way as to stimulate and facilitate defined programmes of social and economic progress.*"

4) V. A. Pai Panandika:

"The key formula of Development Administration can be expressed in the initial letters of Coordination of Resources through Organization of Personnel and Procedures (Cropp)."

2.4.3 Features of Development Administration:

Features of development administration are as follows:

1) **Socio-Economic Development Orientation:**

   One of the defining features of Development Administration is its strong emphasis on socio-economic development. It seeks to address issues such as poverty, inequality, unemployment, and lack of access to basic services by designing and implementing policies that promote economic growth and social progress.

2) **Results-Oriented:**

   Development Administration is results-oriented, focusing on achieving tangible outcomes and measurable improvements in key development indicators. This approach is critical to ensuring that policies and programs have a meaningful impact on the lives of citizens.

3) **Multi-Sectoral Approach:**

   Development challenges are often interconnected and multifaceted. Development Administration recognizes this complexity and takes a multi-sectoral approach, collaborating across various government agencies, international organizations, NGOs, and the private sector to address interconnected issues comprehensively.

4) **Targeted Interventions:**

   Instead of a one-size-fits-all approach, Development Administration tailors interventions to the specific needs and contexts of different regions and communities. This ensures that policies and programs are relevant and effective in addressing local challenges.

5) **Inclusive Governance:**

   Development Administration prioritizes inclusivity in decision-making processes. It engages marginalized and vulnerable groups, such as women, ethnic minorities, and people with disabilities, to ensure that their voices are heard and their needs are met.

6) **Capacity Building:**

   Effective development requires capable institutions and skilled human resources. Development Administration places significant emphasis on building the capacity of government agencies, civil servants, and local communities to plan, implement, and manage development initiatives effectively.

7) **Participatory Approach:**
Engaging citizens in the development process is a hallmark of Development Administration. It encourages citizen participation in policy formulation, project design, and implementation, fostering a sense of ownership and accountability.

8) **Holistic Development:**
Development Administration recognizes that development is not solely economic; it encompasses social, political, and environmental dimensions. It seeks to balance economic growth with social equity, political stability, and environmental sustainability.

9) **Local-Level Empowerment:**
Recognizing the importance of grassroots initiatives, Development Administration empowers local governments and communities to take a proactive role in shaping their own development trajectories. Decentralization and local governance are key components of this approach.

10) **Adaptive and Context-Sensitive:**
Development challenges and contexts vary widely across countries and regions. Development Administration embraces adaptability, recognizing that solutions must be tailored to local realities, cultural norms, and historical legacies.

11) **Public-Private Partnerships:**
Collaboration with the private sector is integral to Development Administration. Public-private partnerships (PPPs) leverage the resources, expertise, and innovation of the private sector to deliver public services, infrastructure, and development projects.

12) **Evidence-Based Policy Making:**
Development Administration places importance on evidence-based decision-making. It relies on data, research, and analysis to formulate policies, monitor progress, and make informed adjustments to development strategies.

2.4.4 Functions of Development Administration:

Here are ten key functions of Development Administration:

1) **Policy Formulation and Planning:**
Development Administration is responsible for formulating development policies and plans that address the socio-economic needs of the country. This involves analyzing data, identifying priorities, and setting goals to guide development efforts.

2) **Resource Allocation and Management:**
Effective resource allocation is crucial for development. Development Administration allocates resources such as budgets, manpower, and infrastructure to various sectors and projects in alignment with development goals.

3) **Project Implementation:**
Development Administration oversees the implementation of development projects, ensuring that they are executed according to plan, on schedule, and within budget. This involves coordinating activities, monitoring progress, and addressing challenges.

4) **Capacity Building:**
Developing countries often require enhanced administrative and technical capacities. Development Administration focuses on building the skills and capabilities of public officials, institutions, and local communities to effectively manage and implement development initiatives.

5) **Public Service Delivery:**
Ensuring access to essential public services is a key function of Development Administration. It works to improve service delivery in areas such as healthcare, education, sanitation, and basic infrastructure to enhance citizens' quality of life.

6) **Stakeholder Engagement:**
Engaging citizens, civil society organizations, the private sector, and international partners is critical in development efforts. Development Administration facilitates dialogue and collaboration among these stakeholders to ensure inclusive decision-making and effective implementation.

7) **Monitoring and Evaluation:**
Development projects and programs must be regularly monitored and evaluated to assess their impact and effectiveness. Development Administration establishes mechanisms to track progress, measure outcomes, and make necessary adjustments.

8) **Poverty Reduction:**
One of the primary goals of Development Administration is poverty reduction. It designs and implements strategies to uplift marginalized and vulnerable populations by creating employment opportunities, providing social safety nets, and promoting inclusive growth.

9) **Institutional Development:**
Strong and efficient institutions are essential for sustainable development. Development Administration focuses on strengthening government agencies, local governments, and regulatory bodies to improve their capacity for effective governance.

10) **Infrastructure and Economic Development:**
Development Administration plays a key role in promoting infrastructure development, including transportation, energy, and communication networks. These infrastructure projects are essential for economic growth and improving the overall business environment.

11) Environmental Sustainability:

Ensuring that development is environmentally sustainable is a critical function. Development Administration integrates environmental considerations into policies and projects, balancing economic growth with conservation efforts.

12) Social Inclusion:

Development Administration seeks to reduce social inequalities and promote social inclusion. It implements programs and policies that address discrimination, empower marginalized groups, and provide equal opportunities for all citizens.

13) Conflict Resolution and Peacebuilding:

In countries affected by conflicts or instability, Development Administration plays a role in post-conflict reconstruction, promoting peace, and addressing the root causes of conflict.

14) Technology and Innovation:

Harnessing technology and promoting innovation are important for development. Development Administration fosters innovation in sectors such as agriculture, healthcare, and education to improve productivity and service delivery.

Review Questions

Q.1. Write Long Answers :

1) Explain the Meaning and Features of System Theory.
2) Discuss the Importance of System Theory.
3) Explain the Meaning and Elements of Rational Choice Theory.
4) Discuss the Importance of Rational Choice Theory.
5) What is Comparative Public Administration? Explain the Nature and Scope of Comparative Public Administration.
6) State the Importance of Comparative Public Administration.
7) What is Development Administration? Explain the Features of Development Administration.
8) Explain the Functions of Development Administration.

Q.2. Short Notes :

1) Principles of System Theory.
2) Limitations of System Theory.
3) Limitations of Rational Choice Theory.
4) Comparative Public Administration.
5) Development Administration.

UNIT 3 New Trends in Public Administration

Introduction:

The emerging new trend in public administration is New Public Management. This NPM concept focuses on result orientation, transparency and accountability of administrative services. Performance management is key to the result orientation. Performance Management system is the record of inputs, processes, outputs and outcome of the procedures of the government. It helps to evaluate and monitor the progress of the government towards the achievement of objectives. In India we don't have Performance Management system. We have conventional tools to manage performance that is performance Appraisal that is mainly based on budgetary allocation and utilization of funds. This paper analyzes the recommendations of second ARC report on performance appraisal system its limitations and how PMS will help to improve the civil services in India the new reforms in public administration is adaption of New Public Management principles in an administration. These principles mainly focus on result orientation, transparency and accountability of administrative services. Performance management is key to the result orientation.

3.1 New Public Management:

The term new public management was coined by scholars from UK and Australia, who were working in the in the areas of public administration. Now, the origin of this new term was to propose a new point of view towards the organizational design in the public sector, however after a decade, the meaning of this term in discussions and debates became many. Some scholars choose to define it as the introduction of new institutional economics to public management and some used it to refer to pattern changes in policy making. Before we make an effort to further understand the various aspects of New Public Management, let us see how it is different from the traditional public administration. The new public management which emerged in the 1980s represented an attempt to make the public sector more businesslike and to improve the efficiency of the Government borrowed ideas and management models from the private sector. It emphasized the centrality of citizens who were the recipient of the services or customers to the public sector.

3.1.1 Meaning:

New Public Management (NPM) is an approach to running public service organizations that is used in government and public service institutions and agencies, at both sub-national and national levels. The term was first introduced by academics in the UK and Australia to describe approaches that were developed during the 1980s as part of an effort to make the public service more "businesslike" and to improve its efficiency by using private sector management models. As with the private sector, which focuses on "customer service", NPM reforms often focused on the "centrality of citizens who were the recipient of the services or customers to the public sector". NPM reformers experimented with using decentralized service delivery models, to give local agencies more freedom in how they delivered programs or services. In some cases, NPM reforms that used e-government consolidated a program or service to a central location to reduce costs.

3.1.2 Definitions:

Here are a few definitions by prominent authors:

1) **Christopher Hood:**

   "New Public Management is a loosely coordinated set of ideas and practices intended to bring the language and logic of markets inside government."

2) **Hood and Jackson:**

   "New Public Management is a type of administrative management that stresses the centrality of management as the vehicle for improving public sector performance and the desirability of bringing private sector techniques and disciplines to government."

3) **Osborne and Gaebler:**

   "New Public Management is a process by which public managers become more like business managers in their focus on efficiency, effectiveness, and performance."

3.1.3 Features of New Public Management:

Here are some key features of New Public Management:

1) **Decentralization and Devolution:**
NPM emphasizes decentralizing decision-making authority and giving more autonomy to lower-level units and agencies. This is intended to make organizations more responsive to local needs and enhance accountability at the operational level.

2) **Market Orientation:**
NPM draws inspiration from market principles and introduces market-like mechanisms into public sector operations. This includes competition, consumer choice, and the use of market-driven incentives to improve performance.

3) **Results-Based Management:**
NPM shifts the focus from input-oriented management to outcomes and results. It encourages the setting of clear performance goals, measuring results, and rewarding success.

4) **Managerialism:**
NPM introduces managerial techniques from the private sector to enhance the efficiency and effectiveness of public organizations. This includes performance evaluations, benchmarking, strategic planning, and goal setting.

5) **Customer Focus:**
NPM emphasizes the importance of understanding and meeting the needs of citizens and customers. Public services are designed and delivered with a customer-centric approach, aiming to improve satisfaction and responsiveness.

6) **Contracting and Outsourcing:**
NPM encourages the use of contracting out and outsourcing to deliver public services. This involves engaging private and non-profit organizations to provide services traditionally delivered by government agencies.

7) **Flexibility and Innovation:**
NPM promotes organizational flexibility and encourages experimentation and innovation. It allows public organizations to adapt to changing circumstances and respond to emerging challenges more effectively.

8) **Performance Measurement and Accountability:**
NPM introduces performance measurement systems to assess the efficiency and effectiveness of public services. This data-driven approach enhances accountability and transparency.

9) **Employee Empowerment:**
NPM recognizes the importance of involving employees in decision-making and encourages a more empowered and motivated workforce. This can lead to increased productivity and innovation.

10) Downsizing and Streamlining:

NPM often involves downsizing and streamlining government bureaucracies to reduce inefficiencies and costs. It seeks to make organizations leaner and more responsive to changing demands.

11) User Fees and Cost Recovery:

NPM encourages the introduction of user fees and cost recovery mechanisms in public services. This aims to reduce the burden on public budgets and increase financial sustainability.

12) Performance-Based Incentives:

NPM introduces performance-based incentives to motivate public employees. Rewards are linked to meeting targets and achieving results, promoting a culture of continuous improvement.

3.1.4 Aspects of New Public Management:

NPM was accepted as the "gold standard for administrative reform" in the 1990s. The idea for using this method for government reform was that if the government guided private-sector principles were used rather than rigid hierarchical bureaucracy, it would work more efficiently. NPM promotes a shift from bureaucratic administration to business-like professional management. NPM was cited as the solution for management ills in various organizational context and policy making in education and health care reform. The basic principles of NPM are can best be described when split into seven different aspects elaborated by Christopher Hood in 1991. Hood also invented the term NPM itself. They are the following:

1) **Management**:

Because of its belief in the importance and strength of privatizing government, it is critical to have an emphasis on management by engaging in hands-on methods. This theory allows leaders the freedom to manage freely and open up discretion.

2) **Performance Standards**:

It's important to maintain explicit standards and measures of performance in a workforce. Using this method promotes clarification of goals/intent, targets, and indicators for progression.

3) **Output Controls**:

The third point acknowledges the "shift from the use of input controls and bureaucratic procedures to rules relying on output controls measured by quantitive performance indicators". This aspect requires using performance based assessments when looking to outsource work to private companies/groups.

4) **Decentralization**:

NPM advocates often shifted from a unified management system to a decentralized system in which managers gain flexibility and are not limited to agency restrictions.

5) **Competition**:

This characteristic focuses on how NPM can promote competition in the public sector which could in turn lower cost, eliminate debate and possibly achieve a higher quality of progress/work through the term contacts. Competition can also be found when the government offers contracts to the private sectors and the contract is given in terms of the ability to deliver the service effectively, quality of the goods provided, hence this will increase competition because the other private sector which did not get the contract will make strides to improve the quality and ability thereby facilitating competition.

6) **Private-Sector Management:**

This aspect focuses on the necessity to establish short-term labor contracts, develop corporate plans or business plans, performance agreements and mission statements. It also focuses on establishing a workplace in which public employees or contractors are aware of the goals and intention that agencies are trying to reach.

7) **Cost Reduction:**

The most effective one which has led to its ascent into global popularity focuses on keeping cost low and efficiency high. "Doing more with less" moreover cost reduction stimulates efficiency and is one way which makes it different from the traditional approach of management.

3.1.5 Importance of New Public Management:

Importance of new public management explained with following points:

1) **Enhanced Efficiency and Effectiveness:**

NPM's emphasis on efficiency, streamlined processes, and performance measurement contributes to better resource utilization and service delivery. By adopting business-like practices, public organizations become more effective in achieving their objectives.

2) **Results-Oriented Governance:**

NPM shifts the focus from inputs to outcomes. This approach encourages public organizations to set clear goals, measure their performance, and evaluate their success based on results achieved. This results-oriented mind-set promotes accountability and transparency.

3) **Innovative Service Delivery:**

NPM encourages innovation in service delivery through its customer-centric approach. Public organizations are motivated to find creative solutions to challenges, leading to improved services that better meet the needs of citizens.

4) **Customer Satisfaction:**

   With NPM's emphasis on customer orientation, public services become more responsive to citizens' demands and preferences. This leads to increased customer satisfaction and trust in government services.

5) **Flexibility in Governance:**

   NPM promotes flexibility by empowering public organizations to adapt to changing circumstances quickly. This agility allows governments to respond to emerging challenges, technological advancements, and shifts in public expectations.

6) **Accountability and Transparency:**

   The focus on performance measurement and results enhances accountability and transparency in public administration. Citizens and stakeholders can assess the effectiveness of government actions, fostering greater trust in government institutions.

7) **Private Sector Collaboration:**

   NPM encourages public-private partnerships, outsourcing, and contracting out services to the private sector. This collaboration leverages the expertise and efficiency of the private sector, leading to improved service quality and reduced costs.

8) **Human Resource Management:**

   NPM introduces performance-based incentives for public employees. This motivates the workforce to excel and rewards their contributions, leading to a more engaged and committed workforce.

9) **Cost Reduction and Budget Discipline:**

   Through streamlining processes, reducing bureaucracy, and emphasizing cost-effectiveness, NPM contributes to budget discipline and the efficient allocation of resources. Governments can achieve more with limited resources.

10) **Adaptation to Changing Contexts:**

    In an era of rapid technological advancements and complex global challenges, NPM provides a framework for governments to adapt to evolving contexts. It equips public organizations to respond to new trends, opportunities, and risks effectively.

11) **Empowerment of Local Governments:**

    NPM's decentralization efforts empower local governments with decision-making authority. This leads to tailored solutions that address unique local needs, fostering community engagement and ownership.

12) **Merit-Based Appointments:**

    NPM promotes merit-based appointments and professional management practices in the public sector. This leads to a more qualified and capable workforce, improving the quality of public service delivery.

3.2 Public Choice Approach:

Public choice theory is an economic approach that seeks to understand and analyze public administration and policy-making by applying principles and methods from the field of economics. It focuses on the study of individual behavior and the interactions of various actors in the public sector, including public officials, politicians, and citizens. Public choice theory assumes that individuals act rationally to maximize their own self-interest, and it applies economic concepts, such as incentives, costs, and benefits, to explain public sector decision-making and outcomes.

3.2.1 Meaning of Public Choice:

Public choice theory is an economic-based approach that seeks to apply the principles of economic theory to the study of public administration and public policy. It explores how individuals and groups make decisions in the context of collective decision-making and the allocation of public resources. Public choice theory assumes that individuals are rational actors who act in their own self-interest and seeks to understand how their behavior shapes public policy outcomes. At its core, public choice theory challenges the traditional view of public administration, which often assumes that public officials and politicians act solely in the public interest or for the common good. Instead, public choice theory posits that individuals in the public sector are motivated by self-interest, much like individuals in the private sector. It recognizes that public actors, including bureaucrats, politicians, and voters, have preferences and make choices based on those preferences and the costs and benefits associated with different options.

3.2.2 Key Principles of Public Choice Theory:

Public choice theory in public administration is based on several key principles that provide a framework for understanding and analyzing the behavior of public actors and the outcomes of public decision-making. These principles are derived from economic theory and emphasize the role of self-interest, incentives, and rational decision-making. Here are some of the key principles of public choice theory in public administration:

1) **Rational Self-Interest:**
   Public choice theory assumes that individuals, including public officials and politicians, are motivated by rational self-interest. They make decisions and take actions that they believe will maximize their own well-being or utility. This principle challenges the traditional view that government actors are solely driven by public interest or altruistic motives.
2) **Utility Maximization:**
   Public choice theory views individuals as utility maximizers who seek to achieve their own goals and preferences. Individuals make choices that they believe will

result in the greatest personal benefit or satisfaction, taking into account the costs and benefits associated with different alternatives. This principle applies to both voters and public officials.

3) **Decision-Making under Constraints:**
Public choice theory recognizes that individuals in the public sector face various constraints, such as limited resources, time, and information. Decision-makers must weigh the costs and benefits of different options and make choices that are most favorable to their self-interest within these constraints. This principle acknowledges the practical realities that influence decision-making in public administration.

4) **Incentives and Disincentives:**
Public choice theory emphasizes the role of incentives in shaping behavior. Individuals respond to positive incentives (rewards) and negative incentives (punishments) in their decision-making. The design of institutional structures, policies, and systems of rewards and punishments can influence the behavior of public officials and politicians. This principle highlights the importance of aligning incentives with desired outcomes.

5) **Rent-Seeking Behavior:**
Public choice theory explores the phenomenon of rent-seeking, which refers to individuals or interest groups seeking to gain economic or political benefits from government actions or policies. Public officials may be influenced by special interest groups seeking favorable treatment or policies that benefit them at the expense of the broader public interest. This principle underscores the potential for suboptimal outcomes and inefficiencies in public decision-making.

6) **Voter Rationality and Information:**
Public choice theory examines the behavior of voters and their decision-making process. It assumes that voters are rational actors who make choices based on their self-interest and the perceived costs and benefits of different policy alternatives. The theory also considers the role of imperfect information and how it can affect voter decision-making and electoral outcomes.

7) **Public Choice and Public Policy:**
Public choice theory has implications for public policy analysis. It highlights the importance of analyzing the incentives, motivations, and behavior of public actors in understanding policy outcomes. The theory suggests that policy choices should consider the self-interested behavior of individuals and the potential impact of special interest groups.

3.2.3 Implications of Public Choice Theory:

Public choice theory, with its emphasis on self-interest, rational decision-making, and incentives, has several implications for the field of public administration. These implications shed light on the behavior of public actors, the functioning of public institutions, and the outcomes of public policies and programs. Here are some key implications of public choice theory in public administration:

1) **Understanding Individual Behavior:**

   Public choice theory helps us understand the behavior of individuals in the public sector, including public officials, politicians, and bureaucrats. It recognizes that these individuals are motivated by self-interest and make choices to maximize their own well-being. This understanding helps explain the decisions and actions taken by public actors and provides insights into their motivations and behavior.

2) **Analysis of Decision-Making Processes:**

   Public choice theory provides a framework for analyzing the decision-making processes in public administration. It emphasizes the rational calculation of costs and benefits by decision-makers and the influence of incentives on their choices. By considering the incentives and constraints faced by public actors, we can better understand how decisions are made and why certain policies or programs are favored over others.

3) **Evaluation of Public Policies:**

   Public choice theory offers insights into the evaluation of public policies and programs. It highlights the importance of analyzing the incentives and motivations of various actors involved in the policy process. By considering how different stakeholders may be seeking to maximize their own interests, we can assess the potential impact of policies and identify potential inefficiencies or rent-seeking behavior.

4) **Designing Effective Institutions:**

   Public choice theory suggests that the design of institutions and governance structures can shape the behavior of public actors. It emphasizes the need to align incentives with desired outcomes and to create checks and balances to mitigate the risks of self-interested behavior. By designing institutions that encourage transparency, accountability, and competition, we can promote better decision-making and improve the effectiveness of public administration.

5) **Addressing Rent-Seeking Behavior:**

   Public choice theory draws attention to the phenomenon of rent-seeking, where individuals or interest groups seek to secure benefits for themselves at the expense of the broader public interest. Understanding rent-seeking behavior is crucial in identifying potential inefficiencies and biases in public decision-making. By recognizing and addressing rent-seeking, public administration can strive for more equitable and efficient outcomes.

6) **Enhancing Citizen Engagement:**

Public choice theory recognizes that citizens are rational actors who respond to incentives. It emphasizes the importance of considering citizen preferences and the costs and benefits they perceive in participating in public decision-making processes. By providing mechanisms for citizen engagement, such as participatory budgeting or public consultations, public administration can better align policies with citizen needs and aspirations.

7) **Promoting Efficiency and Accountability:**

Public choice theory underscores the importance of efficiency and accountability in public administration. By aligning incentives and introducing competitive pressures, the theory encourages a focus on delivering quality public services at the lowest possible cost. It emphasizes the need for transparency, monitoring mechanisms, and effective performance evaluation to hold public actors accountable for their actions and outcomes.

3.2.4 Criticisms on Public Choice Theory:

While public choice theory has made significant contributions to the field of public administration, it is not without its criticisms. Critics argue that the theory oversimplifies human behavior, neglects important aspects of public administration, and relies on unrealistic assumptions. Here are some key criticisms of public choice theory in public administration:

1) **Simplified Assumptions:**

Public choice theory is often criticized for its reliance on simplified assumptions about human behavior. It assumes that individuals are solely motivated by self-interest and rationality, overlooking other important factors such as altruism, social norms, and ethical considerations. Critics argue that this narrow view of human behavior fails to capture the complexities and nuances of real-world decision-making.

2) **Lack of Consideration for Public Interest:**

Public choice theory's emphasis on self-interest can lead to a neglect of the public interest. Critics argue that by assuming that individuals in the public sector are solely motivated by personal gain, the theory overlooks the possibility of public officials genuinely seeking to serve the public good. This narrow focus on self-interest can undermine the importance of public service and the broader goals of public administration.

3) **Neglect of Non-Market Values:**

Public choice theory tends to prioritize market-based solutions and overlook the value of non-market aspects of public administration. Critics argue that the theory's focus on efficiency and individual incentives neglects important social, cultural, and ethical dimensions of public decision-making. This narrow perspective may lead to the undervaluation of public goods and services that do not align with market principles.

4) **Unrealistic Assumptions of Rationality:**
Public choice theory assumes that individuals are perfectly rational decision-makers who possess complete information and can accurately calculate costs and benefits. Critics argue that this assumption does not align with the reality of bounded rationality, limited information, and cognitive biases that influence decision-making. Human behavior in public administration is often influenced by heuristics, biases, and organizational constraints.

5) **Ignoring Power Dynamics:**
Critics argue that public choice theory does not adequately consider power dynamics and the unequal distribution of power and resources in society. It fails to address how power asymmetries and the influence of interest groups can shape public decision-making and policy outcomes. This omission limits the theory's ability to account for the ways in which power and politics affect public administration.

6) **Inadequate Treatment of Institutions:**
Public choice theory often overlooks the role of institutions and their impact on decision-making processes. Critics argue that institutions, including legal frameworks, norms, and organizational structures, shape the incentives and behavior of public actors. Failing to consider the influence of institutions can result in an incomplete understanding of public administration and policy-making.

7) **Limited Policy Prescriptions:**
Public choice theory is sometimes criticized for its limited policy prescriptions. Critics argue that the theory's focus on efficiency and market mechanisms may overlook important social and distributive concerns. It may not adequately address issues of inequality, social justice, and the provision of essential public services. This limited policy scope can hinder the theory's applicability to addressing complex societal challenges.

3.3 Globalisation and Public Administration:

In the field of science and technology, many changes have taken place during the last two centuries. These changes have resulted in bringing the changes in aids to trade and interdependence of various countries has also increased. Fastest means of transports and communications have come into existence. In the entire world, the competition has increased as well as expansion of business has become possible. Financial assistance given by developed countries to underdeveloped countries, technology assistance has facilitated development of economies of different countries. The entire world has been converted into single market. Many barriers in the way of international marketing have been removed. Globalisation in the real sense is a way of corporate life which has further made essential the transnationalism of world economy.

3.3.1 Meaning:

Globalisation in simple words means expansion of businesses globally and giving up the consideration of regional or national boundaries for expansion of business activities. In simple words, it means developing a global outlook or approach of business. The word 'Globalisation' shows the 'Broad attitude' and 'Long vision' of entrepreneurs in the market. It is in other words the removal of short-sighted approach, irrespective of the number of difficulties business are required to face in routine life.

3.3.2 Definitions:

The following are the definitions of globalisation:

1) **Shrawan Kumar Singh :**

   "Globalisation means the global reach of capital to all the world's resources and markets."

2) **Russi Mody :**

   "Globalisation in two way traffic: first it means free competition, high productivity using new technology and second, selling goods in a single market of the whole world."

3) **International Monetary Fund :**

   "Globalisation is the growing economic interdependence of countries worldwide through increasing volume and variety of cross border transactions in goods and services and of international capital flows and also through the more rapid and widespread diffusion of technology."

4) **Anthony McGrew's :**

   "Globalisation is 'an historical process which engenders a significant shift in the spatial reach of networks and systems of social relations to transcontinental or interregional patterns of human organization, activity and the exercise of power.

3.3.3 Challenges of Globalisation before Public Administration:

Globalization, characterized by increased interconnectedness and interdependence among countries, has brought about significant challenges for public administration. Public administration, as the mechanism through which governments implement policies and deliver services, faces a range of complex issues arising from the globalized environment. Here are some key challenges posed by globalization before public administration:

1) **Complex Policy Challenges:**
Globalization has given rise to new and complex policy challenges that cross national boundaries. Public administrators must grapple with issues such as climate change, transnational crime, terrorism, and infectious diseases that require international cooperation and coordination.

2) **Global Economic Integration:**
The global economy's interconnectedness and interdependence have implications for economic policy. Public administrators need to navigate the complexities of trade agreements, currency fluctuations, and global financial crises that impact domestic economies.

3) **Regulatory Harmonization:**
As countries engage in international trade and cooperation, public administrators face challenges in harmonizing regulations and standards across borders to ensure the safety, quality, and fairness of products and services.

4) **Technology and Data Management:**
The digital age has led to the rapid flow of information, raising concerns about data privacy, cybersecurity, and the management of cross-border data flows. Public administrators must develop strategies to safeguard sensitive information and maintain citizens' trust.

5) **Public Health and Pandemics:**
The global movement of people and goods increases the risk of infectious disease outbreaks and pandemics. Public administrators need to develop effective strategies for surveillance, response, and cooperation with international health organizations.

6) **Human Trafficking and Migration:**
Globalization has facilitated human trafficking and irregular migration, leading to challenges related to border security, human rights, and humanitarian crises. Public administrators must address these issues while upholding ethical standards.

7) **Environmental Sustainability:**
Global environmental challenges, such as climate change and pollution, require coordinated efforts among countries. Public administrators play a crucial role in implementing sustainable policies and encouraging international cooperation.

8) **Cultural Diversity and Identity:**
As societies become more diverse due to globalization, public administrators must address issues related to cultural integration, social cohesion, and the protection of minority rights.

9) **Erosion of National Sovereignty:**
Globalization can challenge the traditional concept of national sovereignty as decisions made in one country can have far-reaching effects on others. Public

administrators must strike a balance between national interests and international cooperation.

10) **Inequality and Social Justice:**

Globalization can exacerbate inequalities within and between countries. Public administrators need to develop policies that promote inclusive growth, address disparities, and ensure equitable access to opportunities.

11) **Policy Inertia and Adaptation:**

Traditional bureaucratic structures and slow decision-making processes in public administration may hinder the timely response to rapidly changing global challenges, leading to policy inertia.

12) **Loss of Local Control:**

In a globalized world, decisions made at international levels can have a direct impact on local communities. Public administrators must navigate the tension between global influences and local autonomy.

13) **Capacity and Expertise:**

Addressing global challenges often requires specialized expertise and capacity-building. Public administrators may need to enhance their skills in areas such as international law, diplomacy, and cross-cultural communication.

14) **Political and Ideological Differences:**

International cooperation can be hindered by political and ideological differences among countries. Public administrators must navigate diplomatic complexities to foster collaboration and reach agreements.

15) **Coordination and Collaboration:**

Global challenges often require multi-agency and cross-border collaboration. Public administrators need to overcome bureaucratic silos and foster effective coordination both domestically and internationally.

3.4 Liberalisation and Public Administration:

Many countries in the recent past 1991 onwards have signed GATT agreement, and made possible free movement of goods and services all over the world. Many countries (including India) have principally agreed for the 'free entry' of foreign goods, and foreign companies in local market. India, as one of the members of GATT in recent years is required to adopt the policy of liberalisation and remove all the barriers, restrictions on import export trade activities. The adoption of the policy of liberalisation has made some effects on business and industrial enterprises.

3.4.1 Meaning:

Liberalisation means to reduce unnecessary restrictions and controls on business units imposed by government. It means procedural simplification relaxing trade and industry from unnecessary bureaucratic hurdles. Prior to 1991, government had imposed several types of controls on Indian economy, e.g., industrial licensing system; price control or financial control on goods, import licence, foreign exchange control, restrictions on investment by big business houses, etc. It was experienced by the government that several shortcomings had crept into the economy on account of these controls. These had dampened the enthusiasm of the entrepreneurs to establish new industries. These controls had given rise to corruption, undue delays and inefficiency. Rate of economic growth of the economy fell sharply and high-cost economic system came into being. Economic reforms therefore made a bid to reduce restrictions imposed on the economy.

3.4.2 Definitions:

The following are the definitions of liberalisation:

1) **Dr. V. N. Atri:**

   "Economic liberalisation means more extensive use of the price mechanism that would reduce the anti - export bias of the trade regime. The distortions in the economy should be minimized, if not fully abolished in order to increase efficiency and competition in the economy."

2) **Classical Economists:**

   "The economic policy which leads to reduction if not removal of barriers in the working of market mechanism and free competition is called economic liberalisation."

3.4.3 Challenges of Liberalisation before Public Administration:

Liberalization, often associated with economic reforms, deregulation, and opening up markets, has posed significant challenges for public administration across the globe. The process of liberalization aims to promote economic growth, attract investment, and enhance competitiveness, but it also introduces complexities that public administrators must navigate. As governments reduce their role in certain economic activities, public administration faces a range of challenges that require careful consideration and strategic management. Here are some key challenges of liberalization before public administration:

1) **Balancing Public and Private Interests:**

   Liberalization often involves allowing private entities greater participation in sectors traditionally managed by the public sector. Public administrators must strike a balance between facilitating private sector growth and protecting public interests, such as access to essential services, social welfare, and equitable distribution of benefits.

2) **Regulatory Oversight:**

   As markets are liberalized, regulatory frameworks must evolve to ensure fair competition, consumer protection, and adherence to safety and environmental standards. Public administrators face the challenge of designing effective regulatory mechanisms that prevent abuse of market power and maintain a level playing field.

3) **Capacity Building:**

   The transition to a liberalized economy demands a capable and skilled public administration. Administrators need to develop new competencies to manage the complexities of market-driven policies, regulatory enforcement, and public-private partnerships.

4) **Policy Coordination:**

   Liberalization often involves multiple ministries and agencies working together to implement coherent policies. Public administrators must enhance interagency coordination to prevent conflicting regulations and ensure a comprehensive approach to liberalization.

5) **Privatization and State-Owned Enterprises:**

   Privatizing state-owned enterprises requires careful planning to ensure transparency, fairness, and efficient transfer of assets. Public administrators need to manage the transition while safeguarding public assets and promoting competition.

6) **Labor Market Dynamics:**

   Liberalization can impact labor markets through increased competition, technological changes, and shifts in demand for certain skills. Public administrators must consider policies to retrain workers, protect labor rights, and address potential unemployment challenges.

7) **Social Safety Nets:**

   As markets open up, vulnerable populations might be disproportionately affected by economic shifts. Public administrators need to design and implement social safety nets that provide support to those adversely affected by liberalization.

8) **Fiscal Challenges:**

   Liberalization may lead to reduced government revenue from sectors that were previously monopolized or heavily regulated. Public administrators must identify alternative revenue sources and ensure fiscal sustainability amid changing economic conditions.

9) **Public-Private Partnerships (PPPs):**

   PPPs are often promoted as a way to leverage private sector expertise and resources for public projects. However, public administrators must carefully negotiate and manage PPP contracts to ensure value for money, accountability, and the public interest.

10) **Transparency and Corruption:**

The increased role of the private sector can heighten the risk of corruption. Public administrators must implement robust anti-corruption measures and ensure transparency in procurement, licensing, and regulatory processes.

11) **Public Services:**

Liberalization can impact the quality and accessibility of public services such as healthcare, education, and utilities. Public administrators must develop strategies to maintain essential services and ensure they remain accessible to all citizens.

12) **Capacity for Negotiation:**

When negotiating trade agreements and international economic treaties, public administrators must have the capacity to protect national interests, including intellectual property rights, environmental standards, and public health.

13) **Environmental Concerns:**

Liberalization can lead to increased resource consumption and environmental degradation. Public administrators must incorporate sustainable development principles into policies and regulations to mitigate negative environmental impacts.

14) **Local and Regional Disparities:**

The benefits of liberalization might not be evenly distributed across regions. Public administrators must address regional disparities and implement targeted policies to promote equitable development.

15) **Political Acceptance and Communication:**

The changes associated with liberalization can face resistance from stakeholders who fear job losses, increased inequality, or loss of cultural identity. Public administrators must engage in effective communication and build political consensus to gain public acceptance.

3.5 Privatisation and Public Administration:

The economic policy of 1991 introduced reforms to 'reform' the public enterprises. Government decided to reduce the number of industries reserved for the public sector and the disinvestment of shares of a selected set of public sector enterprises. Government also decided to reduce drastically the budgetary support to sick PSUs. Thus, privatisation would mean here the introduction of private ownership in PSUs. Privatisation reduces the involvement of the state in the nation's economic activities. In the context of economic reforms, privatisation means allowing the private sector to set up more and more of such industries as were previously reserved for public sector. Under it, existing enterprises of the public sector are either wholly or partially sold to private sector. It enhances the importance of private sector because private sector comes to play significant role in the economic development of the country. Thus, transferring of public sector industries to private sector is called privatisation.

3.5.1 Meaning:

Privatisation means transfer of ownership and / or management of an enterprise private sector. It also means the withdrawal of the state from an industry or sector, partially or fully. Another dimension of privatisation is opening up of an industry that has been reserved for the public sector to the private sector. In a broader sense, privatisation is something more than mere transfer of ownership from Government to private people. Privatisation involves deregulation opening of the economic for a free play of the market forces and transfer of shares to the general public.

3.5.2 Definitions:

The following are the definitions of privatisation:

1) **Barbara Lee and John Nelis :**

   "Privatisation is the general process of involving the private sector in the ownership or operation of a state owned enterprise."

2) **D. R. Pendse :**

   "Privatisation is a process which reduces the involvement of state or public sector in country's economic activity."

3) **J .N. Goodrich :**

   "Privatisation refers to any process that results in the transfer of functions, activities, assets or organisation in whole or in part which is owned or controlled either directly or indirectly by the Government to a non government body."

3.5.3 Challenges of Privatisation before Public Administration:

Privatization, the process of transferring ownership and control of public assets and services to the private sector, has become a prominent economic reform strategy adopted by governments around the world. While privatization is often pursued to improve efficiency, reduce government intervention, and attract investment, it presents a range of challenges for public administration. These challenges encompass various aspects of governance, accountability, social welfare, and economic stability.

1) **Loss of Public Control:**

   One of the primary concerns of privatization is the loss of public control over essential services and assets. As services transition to the private sector, public administrators may have limited influence over decisions related to pricing, service quality, and accessibility.

2) **Quality Erosion:**

   Privatization can lead to a focus on profit maximization rather than service quality. Private firms may cut corners, reduce staff, or compromise on standards to increase profitability, resulting in a decline in service quality.

3) **Service Disruptions:**

During the transition from public to private ownership, service disruptions can occur. Public administrators must ensure a seamless transition to prevent interruptions in critical services that affect citizens' daily lives.

4) **Access Inequities:**

Private firms may prioritize areas that are more profitable, leading to unequal access to services across regions. Vulnerable and marginalized communities may face reduced access to essential services, exacerbating social inequalities.

5) **Higher Costs:**

While privatization aims to improve efficiency, it can sometimes result in higher costs for consumers. Private firms may charge higher prices, particularly in sectors where competition is limited or absent.

6) **Job Losses and Labor Conditions:**

Privatization can lead to job losses and deteriorating labor conditions as private firms seek to cut costs. Public administrators must address the social and economic impacts of job displacement and ensure that workers' rights are protected.

7) **Loss of Accountability:**

The accountability of private firms may be different from that of public entities. Private firms are primarily accountable to their shareholders, which may lead to conflicts between profit motives and public welfare.

8) **Monopoly and Oligopoly:**

In sectors with limited competition, privatization can lead to the emergence of monopolies or oligopolies, resulting in reduced consumer choice, higher prices, and abuse of market power.

9) **Corruption and Lack of Transparency:**

The involvement of private entities can lead to a lack of transparency in decision-making processes. Privatization may also create opportunities for corruption, particularly during the bidding and contracting phases.

10) **Short-Term Focus:**

Private firms often prioritize short-term profits over long-term investments. This can lead to neglect of necessary maintenance, research, and development, which may negatively impact the sustainability of services.

11) **Reduced Public Influence:**

As public services are privatized, citizens' ability to influence decisions and policies may diminish. Public administrators must ensure that citizens' voices are heard and that their interests are protected.

12) Financial Constraints:

Governments may face financial constraints as they forgo revenue generated by public assets. This can impact public investment in critical sectors, such as education, healthcare, and infrastructure.

13) Loss of Collective Ownership:

Privatization can erode the sense of collective ownership that citizens have over public assets. Public administrators must consider the social and cultural implications of transferring ownership to the private sector.

Review Questions

Q.1. Write Long Answers :

1) What is New Public Management? Explain the Features of New Public Management.
2) Explain the Importance of New Public Management.
3) Explain the Meaning and Principles of Public Choice Approach.
4) Discuss the Implications of Public Choice Approach.
5) What is Globalisation? Explain the Challenges of Globalisation before Public Administration.
6) What is Liberalisation? Explain its Challenges before Public Administration.
7) What is Privatisation? Discuss the Challenges of Privatisation before Public Administration.
8) Explain how Process of Liberalization and Privatization has affected the Functioning of Public Administration.

Q.2. Short Notes :

1) Aspects of New Public Management.
2) Criticisms on Rational Choice Approach.
3) Globalisation.
4) Privatisation.
5) Liberalisation.

UNIT 4
Governance

Introduction:

Governance in public administration refers to the processes, structures, and mechanisms through which government institutions and officials exercise authority, make decisions, and manage public affairs. It encompasses the principles of transparency, accountability, participation, and responsiveness in the administration of public resources and services. Effective governance involves collaborative interactions between government, civil society, and the private sector, aiming to ensure the efficient, equitable, and ethical delivery of public goods and services, while also addressing societal needs and fostering public trust in the functioning of government.

4.1. Good Governance :

The terms "governance" and "good governance" are being increasingly used in development literature. Bad governance is being increasingly regarded as one of the root causes of all evil within our societies. Major donors and international financial institutions are increasingly basing their aid and loans on the condition that reforms that ensure "good governance" are undertaken. It is also argued that bad governance not only minimises freedom but also denies sustainable economy. In this respect it has been necessary to find out the ills of bad governance and benefits of good governance in relation to the sustainable economic growth.

4.1.1. Meaning :

In international development, good governance is a way of measuring how public institutions conduct public affairs and manage public resources in a preferred way. Governance is "the process of decision-making and the process by which decisions are implemented (or not implemented)". Governance in this context can apply to corporate, international, national, or local governance as well as the interactions between other sectors of society. The concept of "good governance" thus emerges as a model to compare ineffective economies or political bodies with viable economies and political bodies. The concept centers on the responsibility of governments and governing bodies to meet the needs of the masses as opposed to select groups in society. Because countries often described as "most successful" are liberal democratic states, concentrated in Europe and the Americas, good governance standards often measure other state institutions against these states. Aid organizations and the authorities of developed countries often will focus the meaning of "good governance" to a set of requirements that conform to the organization's agenda, making "good governance" imply many different things in many different contexts. The opposite of good governance, as a concept, is bad governance.

4.1.2. Definitions :

Following are the definitions of good governance:

1) **The World Bank:**

   "Good governance is central to creating and sustaining an environment which fosters strong and equitable development and it is an essential complement to sound economic policies".

2) **UNDP:**

   "Good Governance is, among other things, participatory, transparent and accountable. It is also effective and equitable. And it promotes the rule of law. Good governance ensures that political, social, and economic priorities are based on broad consensus in society and that the voices of the poorest and the most vulnerable are heard in decision making over the allocation of development resources"

3) **The International Monetary Fund (IMF):**

   "Good governance is a broad concept covering all aspects of how a country is governed, including its economic policies, regulatory framework, and adherence to rule of law".

4.1.3. Origin and Emergence of the Concept of Good Governance :

"Good governance" was initially expressed in a 1989 World Bank publication. In 1992, the bank published a report entitled, Governance and Development, which explored the concept further and its application. In 1997, the bank redefined the concept "good governance" as a necessary precondition for development. Good governance is to promote and sustain holistic and integrated human development. The central focus is to see how the government enables, simplifies and authorises its people, regardless of differences of caste, creed, class and political ideology and social origin to think and take certain decisions which will be in their best interest and which will enable them to lead a clean, decent, happy and autonomous existence.

4.1.4. Characteristics of Good Governance :

Good governance has 8 major characteristics. It is participatory, consensus oriented, accountable, transparent, responsive, effective and efficient, equitable and inclusive and follows the rule of law. It assures that corruption is minimised, the views of minorities are taken into account and that the voices of the most vulnerable in society are heard in decision-making. It is also responsive to the present and future needs of society.

1) **Participation :**

   Participation by both men and women is a key cornerstone of good governance. Participation could be either direct or through legitimate intermediate institutions or representatives. It is important to point out that representative democracy does not necessarily mean that the concerns of the most vulnerable in society would be taken into consideration in decision-making. Participation needs to be informed and organised. This means freedom of association and expression on the one hand and an organised civil society on the other hand.

2) **Rule of law :**

   Good governance requires fair legal frameworks that are enforced impartially. It also requires full protection of human rights particularly those of minorities. Impartial enforcement of laws requires an independent judiciary and an impartial and incorruptible police force.

3) **Transparency :**

   Transparency means that decisions taken and their enforcement are done in a manner that follows rules and regulations. It also means that information is freely available and directly accessible to those who will be affected by such decisions and their enforcement. It also means that enough information is provided and that it is provided in easily understandable forms and media.

4) **Responsiveness :**

   Good governance requires that institutions and processes try to serve all stakeholders within a reasonable timeframe.

5) **Consensus oriented :**

   There are several actors and as many view-points in a given society. Good governance requires mediation of the different interests in society to reach a broad consensus in society on what is in the best interest of the whole community and how this can be achieved. It also requires a broad and long-term perspective on what is needed for sustainable human development and how to achieve the goals of such development. This can only result from an understanding of the historical, cultural and social contexts of a given society or community.

6) **Equity and inclusiveness :**

A society's well-being depends on ensuring that all its members feel that they have a stake in it and do not feel excluded from the mainstream of society. This requires all groups but particularly the most vulnerable, have opportunities to improve or maintain their well-being.

7) **Effectiveness and efficiency :**

Good governance means that processes and institutions produce results that meet the needs of society while making the best use of resources at their disposal. The concept of efficiency in the context of good governance also covers the sustainable use of natural resources and the protection of the environment.

8) **Accountability :**

Accountability is a key requirement of good governance. Not only governmental institutions but also the private sector and civil society organisations must be accountable to the public and to their institutional stakeholders. Who is accountable to who varies depending on whether decisions or actions taken are internal or external to an organisation or institution. In general, an organisation or an institution is accountable to those who will be affected by its decisions or actions. Accountability cannot be enforced without transparency and the rule of law.

4.1.5 Significance of Good Governance :

The importance of good governance in a state is immense. Sustainable development is not possible without good governance.

1) **Economic Development:**

Without good governance in a state, the economic development of that state is not stable. All elements of economic development, such as production, distribution, investment, and even consumption, face various obstacles. If good governance is established, such obstacles will be removed and the fair distribution of state resources will be possible.

2) **Social Development:**

Good governance is essential for social development. The role of it does not end only with economic development. The result of development ensures that every class of people in society enjoys the basis of fairness. People of different religions, castes, and classes live in a society. Now, if there is no fair distribution of wealth among all these people, social discontent will increase. Again, the proper distribution of wealth is not enough. We have to make arrangements so that the minority people can walk without fear. In the same way, various reform laws have to be enacted to reduce the gap between men and women in society.

3) **Political Development:**

Its relationship with political development is quite important. If the political leaders of a country are not active in establishing good governance, then its establishment in that country is not possible. Its success depends largely on the sincerity of the political leadership and adherence to the rules and regulations of the political establishment. The constructive cooperation between the political institutions and the political parties and the formulation of programs for the welfare of the people play an important role in establishing good competition and good governance among themselves. For example, in a democracy, mutual cooperation between the government and the opposition helps to establish it in the country.

4) **Enhancing Public Trust:**

Good governance builds public trust and confidence in institutions and organizations. When governance processes are transparent, accountable, and inclusive, it fosters trust among citizens, employees, stakeholders, and the general public. This trust is essential for maintaining social cohesion, promoting cooperation, and facilitating the smooth functioning of society.

5) **Promoting Economic Development:**

Good governance is closely linked to economic development and prosperity. Transparent and accountable governance practices attract investments, encourage entrepreneurship, and create an enabling environment for business growth. Effective governance helps to reduce corruption, enhance regulatory frameworks, and promote fair competition, leading to sustainable economic development.

6) **Ensuring Rule of Law:**

Good governance upholds the rule of law and ensures that institutions and individuals are governed by a set of fair and just laws and regulations. It promotes legal and judicial systems that are independent, impartial, and accessible to all citizens. The rule of law provides a foundation for stability, predictability, and protection of individual rights, fostering a conductive environment for social and economic progress.

7) **Improving Service Delivery:**

Good governance is essential for efficient and effective service delivery. It ensures that public resources are allocated and utilized in a transparent, equitable, and accountable manner. Through proper governance mechanisms, public institutions are able to deliver essential services such as education, healthcare, infrastructure, and social welfare programs to the citizens in a timely and responsive manner.

8) **Empowering Citizens and Ensuring Participation:**
Good governance encourages citizen engagement, participation, and empowerment. It ensures that decision-making processes are inclusive, allowing citizens to have a voice in shaping policies and programs that affect their lives. By involving citizens in decision-making, governance fosters a sense of ownership, promotes social cohesion, and enables the integration of diverse perspectives.

9) **Fostering Accountability and Transparency:**
Good governance promotes accountability and transparency in the actions and decisions of public officials and institutions. It establishes mechanisms for oversight, monitoring, and evaluation to ensure that public resources are used efficiently and for the intended purposes. Transparency in governance processes enables citizens to hold public officials accountable for their actions, thereby reducing corruption and enhancing public trust.

10) **Managing Conflict and Promoting Peace:**
Good governance plays a crucial role in managing conflicts and promoting peace within societies. By providing fair and impartial systems for resolving disputes, ensuring equitable distribution of resources, and promoting inclusivity, governance contributes to social stability and peaceful coexistence. It helps to address grievances, reduce inequalities, and build mechanisms for dialogue and reconciliation.

11) **Protecting Human Rights:**
Good governance safeguards and promotes human rights. It ensures that individuals are treated with dignity, equality, and respect, and that their fundamental rights are protected. Effective governance systems uphold principles such as non-discrimination, freedom of expression, access to justice, and respect for human dignity, creating an environment where human rights are respected and upheld.

4.2. Corruption :

Corruption affects every society in some or the other way. But, in developing societies like India, it has assumed such tendencies that many other problems have become dependent on it. In fact, the whole programme of development has been severely paralyzed by bureaucratic malpractices. Today, no country can claim to be completely free from corruption, but every country tries to keep it at bare minimum level so that it does not affect much. The concept of corruption is closely integrated with the concept of integrity.

4.2.1 Meaning:

Corruption refers to the abuse of entrusted power for personal gain or to gain an unfair advantage. It involves dishonest or unethical conduct by individuals, often public officials or those in positions of authority, who use their influence, authority, or resources for personal enrichment or to manipulate systems for their own benefit. Corruption can take various forms, such as bribery, embezzlement, nepotism, fraud, and abuse of power and it undermines the principles of transparency, fairness, accountability, and integrity in both public and private sectors. It has detrimental effects on society, the economy, governance, and overall development, eroding public trust, distorting markets, and hindering progress.

4.2.2 Definitions:

Following are the definitions of corruption:

1) **Transparency International:**
   "Corruption is the abuse of entrusted power for private gain. It can be classified as grand, petty, and political, depending on the amounts of money lost and the sector where it occurs."
2) **Rose-Ackerman:**
   "Corruption occurs when an agent, such as a public official, politician, or private individual, who is entrusted with power on behalf of the public interest, breaches that trust for personal gain."
3) **Susan Rose-Ackerman:**
   "Corruption refers to the misuse of public power, office, or resources by government officials or employees who exchange favours for personal gain."
4) **Johnston:**
   "Corruption is any behaviour by officials in the public or private sector in which they improperly and unlawfully enrich themselves, or those close to them, by misuse of the position in which they are placed."

4.2.3 Causes of Corruption:

India's per capita Gross Domestic Product (GDP) in 2015 places it among the ranks of the world's lower middle-income countries. Given the inverted-U shaped relationship between corruption and per capita GDP across countries, it seems intuitive that corruption in India might pose a particular challenge. In the poorest countries, corruption is limited because there is, frankly, not much to steal; in the most undeveloped economies, there is little need to delegate the types of discretionary tasks that lend themselves to bribery. On the opposite end of the spectrum, the rich, advanced industrialized countries have developed robust legal frameworks and institutional and enforcement mechanisms necessary to deter and combat corruption. As Laffont (2006) points out, one is likely to find the greatest corruption in those countries standing at the unfortunate juncture of a heavily regulated economy that does not yet boast adequate enforcement capacity

1) **Lack of Effective Management and Organisation:**

Due to mismanagement and misorganisation, there is a weak control on various departments and their working. This leads to lack of coordination and control among departments and levels of organisation. This uncontrolled and unsupervised administration gives rise to corruption on large scale. Besides, appointment of inefficient and incapable managers and executives on various levels of hierarchy also leads to mismanagement and misorganisation. The only cause of this wrong appointment is corruption. Hence, corruption breeds corruption.

2) **Lack of Economical Stability:**

Economical crisis and price hike are major causes of corruption. Economical crisis leads to unemployment and change in standard of living. It develops a feeling of insecurity in the minds of affected people. Most of the people do not have patience and courage to face this situation. In order to regain their employment and to maintain standard of living and status, this affected people engage themselves in illegal and immoral activities. They do not want to work hard again for achieving the same position and post. They use various illegal short cuts for achieving them.

3) **Lack of Effective Leadership:**

Good leaders can only lead people towards growth, development and progress. They play significant role in eradication of social evils. In India, there is tremendous shortage of good leaders. Leaders convey message of citizens to the administration and government. They lead the people against corruption and social evils. A country cannot survive without honest and sincere leaders. There is urgent need of leaders like Mahatma Gandhiji. We need more Anna Hazares and Medha patkars.

4) **Lack of Support:**

There are few good leaders in India. They strive hard to eradicate corruption from the society. But due to lack of support and cooperation from people, the voice and efforts of these great leaders are often suppressed. People of India are more concerned with their life than the development and protection of their country against social evils. Many citizens have accepted corruption as a part of their life. They think, it is useless and waste of time, to support leaders against corruption.

5) **Lack of Values:**

Home and educational institution play a significant role in character building of citizens. Moral values are only taught in most of these institutions. But, they are not properly inculcated in individual. This is the basic cause of corruption. Many parents and teachers do not practice what they preach. Hence, their preaching does not bring out desired results. Children imitate parents. If parents are corrupt, it is more likely that children will also become corrupt.

6) **Lack of Love for Country:**
Due to rapid modernization and globalization, people are becoming more and more selfish. They are only concerned with self enrichment and wealth accumulation. The only objective of many Indian is to become rich as soon as possible. They consider themselves as patriotic just by celebrating independence and republic day. They do not know the actual meaning of patriotism. They are not concerned with development of nation and rights of others. Due to this attitude, they easily get involved in corruption and immoral activities. During strike and protests, many politically affiliated citizen's damage and destroy public property.

7) **Lack of Proper System:**
In India, corruption exists in all levels and areas of system. Very few honest people survive in this corrupt system. Those who raise their voice against corruption are killed or forced to resign. This accelerates the growth of corruption. Most of the people involved in Indian system have take corruption as part and parcel of their duties. They don't have hatred or ill feeling towards corruption. They think that without it, we cannot survive and sustain in this system. Besides, systems are interrelated and interdependent. As a result, corruption spreads like tumour in all the systems.

8) **Lack of Satisfaction:**
Greed results from non-satisfaction. People are not satisfied with their current status, position and wealth. They want to become millionaire in a short span of time. Growth and richness is not bad. But it is sad to see that the Indian are adopting illegal and immoral ways to achieve them. Many Indians are engaged in unhealthy competitions of wealth accumulation (with relatives, colleagues and neighbours).

9) **Lack of Autonomy:**
Establishment and expansion of private and business sector depend on approval of politician. Many politician misuse their authority and power. They have only one criterion for approval "Pay us otherwise you will not get paid". Entrepreneurs consider bribery as tax like other official taxes. Bribery has become necessary for the establishment of organisation. Companies and contractors secure contracts and government projects due to bribe. Good quotations and work of company does not considered to be criteria for securing contracts.

10) **Lack of Good Control and Vigilance:**
In India, some agencies are working day and night to stop corruption. But some officials of these agencies get tempted towards illegal commissions and leave corrupt people without any penalty and punishment. Corruption breeds corruption. To keep a check on crores of people, more agencies and more honest officials are required. Hence, there is a tremendous shortage of these agencies and officials in India. This results in lack of control and vigilance on illegal activities.

11) Lack of Good Remuneration:

In private sector, employer decides salary and employment benefits. He has complete freedom and there is no pressure on him from government. Due to this fact, many employers pay less for more work. They exploit employees of their companies. Even the working conditions in most of the establishments are worse. Employee does not have any social security and retirement benefits. Employees get frustrated and adopt illegal means to make their earnings better and future secure.

12) Lack of employment:

Many unemployed educated youth fall prey to corruption. They are willing to pay huge amount for jobs. Many employer take undue advantage of this situation. They take bribe and give appointment letters. The appointed employee uses all means (legal and illegal) to recover his lost money as early as possible. Hence, Corruption breeds corruption. When these employees achieve power and authority. They take bribe from candidates for jobs. This tradition of corruption continues from generation to generation without any check and control.

13) Lack of Seats and Educational Institutions:

In order to fulfill dreams and ambitions of their children, parents pay huge donation to secure admission for their children. Hence, the basis of admission is not merit but money. Management use maximum utilization of quota granted to them. Every year there is an increase in donation amount. Affluent students who secured less percentage in examinations, easily gets admissions by paying huge donations. Poor students who secured good percentage struggle day and night to get admissions. Many a time their efforts go in vain due to lack of seats and more number of applicants.

4.2.4 Impact of Corruption:

In 1997, Tanzi and Davoodi conducted a systematic study of the impact of corruption on public finances. Several important findings came to light: Corruption increases the volume of public investments (at the expense of private investments), as there are many options that allow for public expenditure manipulation and are carried out by high-level officials so as to get bribes (which means that more general government expenditures or a large budget offer more opportunities for corruption). Corruption redirects the composition of public expenditure from the expenditure necessary for basic functioning and maintenance to expenditure on new equipment.

1) Loss of National Wealth:

This is the greatest loss for the people of India. Since independence, India is showing tremendous growth in corruption (Jeep deal to 2 G spectrum scams). India lost billions and billions dollars of money in various scams. Instead of becoming independent affluent nation, India is dependent on international loans, grants and favours due to this tremendous of wealth in corruption.

2) Hindrance and Obstruction in Development:

Corruption is the only obstruction in the way towards development. We cannot become a developed and self sufficient nation until corruption is not eradicated from our country. Many developmental projects are taking unnecessary time for their completion due to corruption. Since, many officials consider these projects as special hens (hens which lay golden eggs every day). If project will get completed, these special hens will die. Hence, they take proper care of these hens.

3) Backwardness:

Due to corruption, India is behind in almost every field- sports, inventions, health, medicine, research, education, economy, defence, infrastructure, technology and so on. Many scientists do not have latest equipments and technology for research and development. Sportsmen do not have proper facilities, equipments, coaching and training. There are scams and corruption in defence deals. Many doctors lack specialized and modern skills of treatment and diagnosis.

4) Poverty:

Due to corruption, government is unable to eradicate poverty. Rich are becoming richer by snatching the rights and wealth of poor. Various packages, reservations and compensations for poor people, minorities and backward community are announced by government from time to time. But these disadvantaged sections of society hardly get any benefits. Since, affluent people freely consume benefits meant for poor.

5) Authority and Power in Wrong Hands:

Ineligible and incapable candidates are selected for various important positions. They pay and get selected. Due to their inefficiency, there exist many faults and weaknesses in system and management.These faults get easily hidden through corruption. The deserving and creative candidates satisfy themselves with unsuitable jobs and positions.

6) Brain Drain:

Corrupt employers and mediators offer jobs to unskilled and incapable candidates by taking bribe. They get their share of wealth. But nation loses its valuable share. Due to lack of good opportunities in India, many creative and talented Indian are serving developed nations. This is a tremendous loss for India. Since, we cannot become a developed nation without the contribution of talented and creative people. Talented people who serve other countries are actually cheating with their own nation. They are made capable and efficient by their own nation. But they use their capabilities for increasing the efficiency of other nation. This is also considered as corruption.

7) Rise in Terrorism and Crimes:

One of the reasons for rise in crimes is corruption in police administration. Police departments grant security and protection to the citizens. When this departments get engaged in corrupt activities. Then there is no control on crimes and brutal killings. Since, criminals are given freedom and victims are tortured. Besides, corruption also leads to injustice. Injustice gives birth to crimes and anti social activities. Citizens take up arms for securing justice.

8) Rise in Suicide Cases:

Suicide cases are increasing in India by leaps and bounds. One of the major causes in several suicide cases is injustice resulting from corruption. Government announces various schemes and help packages for farmers but most of the time this financial help does not reach to the farmers due to corruption in administration. This leads to rise suicides cases among farmers. Candidates fulfill all necessary criteria for jobs or admissions, but then also they fail in their attempt to secure it. Because they do not have political contacts and money. This leads to hopelessness and depression which ultimately results in suicide.

9) Psychological and Social Disorders:

Due to corruption in judicial system and police administration. Culprits are left free and victims get punishments and injustice. Due to this injustice, many victims suffer from depression and serious psychological disorders. Many victims get frustrated with judicial system and develop feeling of revenge against culprits. As results, the victims become culprits by engaging themselves in anti-social activities. It corrodes the healthy social fabric of nation.

4.2.5 Prevention of Corruption in India:

Prevention of corruption in India is given below:

1) Value Education:

Parents and teachers should inculcate moral values in children. Practice is more persuasive than preaching. The best way to inculcate values in children is not only to preach but to set an example by actual doing. They should set themselves as models of good behaviour. They should narrate stories based on moral values. Teacher should not only teach morals in value education period but they should inculcate values in pupils by correlating value education with various subjects and activities. They should not leave any stone unturned for achieving this great purpose.

2) Effective and Regular Vigilance:

Strict action should be taken against lazy and corrupt officials. Number of agencies and officials should be increased. They should be properly trained in the latest investigative skills. Government should supervise and monitor these agencies. They should be quick and active in their duties. They should not delay their investigation and inspection .Since, this delay is the cause for loss of tremendous wealth of nation.

3) **Responsible Citizen:**
If an individual is corrupt, he cannot expect those in power to be free from corruption. Hence, it is essential for every citizen to perform his duties faithfully and to the best of their abilities. Every citizen should strive hard to eradicate corruption. People of India should report cases of corruption to vigilance department immediately without delay. They should follow up the cases of corruption. Since, merely reporting the evil practice is not sufficient for its complete eradication.

4) **Strong and Effective Leadership and Administration:**
All those who are granted powers and authority by people should fulfill their promises and pledge. They should strive their utmost to eradicate corruption from systems and administrations. They should give up hypocrisy. Government and vigilance agencies should keep a check on their source of income and bank accounts. If any leader is not performing his duties properly, then he should be immediately terminated from the position. It should be performance based position. Government should do performance appraisal of leaders regularly.

5) **Media:**
Media has wider coverage and impact. It plays an important role in changing the life of people. It should frequently expose the cases of corruption. It should educate people against corruption on regular basis. Journalists and editors should give complete information about the issues related to corruption in their newspapers. Reporters should give more importance to the news and information on corruption; they should report corruption cases immediately.

6) **Legislation:**
Government should frame strict and stringent anti-corruption laws. Severe punishments and penalties should be imposed on corrupt people. The justice and proceedings should not be delayed. Immediate action should be taken against corrupt people. The punishment should act as a good lesson for other corrupt people.

7) **Social organisation:**
Non government organizations should work in coordination with people and vigilance departments for prevention of illegal activities. They should devise and plan innovative strategies and methods against corruption.

8) **Declaration of Wealth and Assets:**
It should be made mandatory for political leaders and government officials to declare their wealth and assets. Investigation agencies should strictly and properly check their claims and declaration.

9) **Transparency:**
Every process of selection, dealing and appointments of different fields should be made transparent. People should be made aware of reasons and merit for selection of candidates, contracts, tenders, etc.

10) **Advertising:**
Advertising and marketing agencies should educate and aware people against corruption. There should be appealing ads on internet, vehicles, bus stops, railway stations, sign boards and television.

11) **Serials and films:**
Films are powerful medium of mass communication. Films have powerful influence and widespread appeal. Films can be used to create public opinion against corruption. Producers should make certain popular serials and movies against corruption. Serials should have different episodes dealing with various types of corruption and their cures.

12) **Appointment and admissions:**
Selection of students, managers, officers and executives should only be based on merit. It is the responsibility of candidates and parents to critically examine the selection and appointment procedures. They should report irregularities to the higher authorities without delay.

13) **Religious sermon:**
In India, people show very strict adherence to their faith and belief. They are very sensitive towards religion, place of worship and religious leaders. They have deep attachment and great respect for preachers and spiritual orators. They try to adopt the teachings of their spiritual leaders in day to day life. Hence, religious leaders should give sermons against corruption.

14) **Loyalty and patriotism:**
Every citizen of India should become patriotic in true sense. He should give priority and preference to the development of his nation. He should always remain loyal to their beautiful culture, ethics and country. Social workers, political leaders, media and teachers should inculcate true patriotism in the citizens of India.

4.3 Ombudsman:

An ombudsman, also known as an ombudsperson or ombuds, is an independent and impartial official who is appointed to investigate and address complaints and grievances from individuals or groups regarding the actions, decisions, or practices of government agencies, organizations, or institutions. The role of an ombudsman is to act as a mediator and advocate for fairness, transparency, and accountability in administrative processes. Ombudsmen are typically tasked with ensuring that individuals' rights are protected, addressing instances of maladministration, and promoting good governance practices.

4.3.1 Meaning of Ombudsman:

The term "ombudsman" originates from the Swedish word "ombudsman," which means "representative" or "agent." An ombudsman is an independent and impartial official appointed to investigate and address complaints and grievances from individuals or groups regarding the actions, decisions, or practices of government agencies, organizations, or institutions. The role of an ombudsman is to act as a mediator and advocate for fairness, transparency, and accountability in administrative processes. Ombudsmen provide an avenue for individuals to voice their concerns, seek redress for grievances, and receive assistance in navigating bureaucratic systems, often without the need for formal legal proceedings. Ombudsmen play a crucial role in promoting good governance, protecting individual rights, and ensuring that administrative processes adhere to established laws and ethical standards.

4.3.2 Origin of Ombudsman:

Sweden is a native land of the institution of Ombudsman." In 1713 King Charles XII of Sweden, had been out of the country at war with Russia for nearly twelve years. He gave order for the appointment of a supreme representative of the King known as Hogste Ombudsman." This institution was established by the King to ensure effective enforcement of law and order and to observe the functioning of the public servants and also to see that they discharged their duties in the public interest. In 1719, the name of the Hogste Ombudsman was changed and became Justitie Kansler. But the functions, duties and responsibilities of the Justitie Kanter did not undergo any significant change. But during 1766 to 1772 his position was changed and his appointment was made by the existing representative bodies and not by the King of Sweden."

4.3.3 Functions of Ombudsman:

The office of the Ombudsman is established to uphold transparency, accountability, and fairness in administrative processes, and it wields certain powers and functions to achieve these goals. These powers and functions vary depending on the jurisdiction and the specific mandates of the Ombudsman. Here are key powers and functions commonly associated with the office of the Ombudsman:

1) **Investigation of Complaints:**

   One of the primary functions of the Ombudsman is to investigate complaints from individuals or groups who believe they have been subjected to unfair treatment, maladministration, or abuse of power by government agencies, organizations, or institutions. The Ombudsman thoroughly examines the complaint, gathers evidence, and seeks to find a just resolution.

2) **Mediation and Conflict Resolution:**

The Ombudsman serves as a mediator between complainants and the relevant authorities. By facilitating dialogue and negotiation, the Ombudsman seeks to find mutually agreeable solutions to disputes, avoiding the need for formal legal proceedings and promoting amicable resolutions.

3) **Recommendations:**

Based on the findings of investigations, the Ombudsman has the power to make recommendations to rectify injustices, address systemic issues, and improve administrative processes. These recommendations may include changes in policies, procedures, or practices to prevent similar issues from arising in the future.

4) **Transparency and Accountability:**

The Ombudsman ensures that administrative actions are transparent and accountable by examining decisions, procedures, and practices for compliance with laws, regulations, and ethical standards. This function helps prevent abuse of power and promotes public trust in government institutions.

5) **Access to Information:**

Ombudsmen often have the authority to access information and documents relevant to their investigations, even if such information is otherwise considered confidential. This power ensures that the Ombudsman can thoroughly examine the evidence and make informed decisions.

6) **Systemic Review:**

Beyond individual complaints, the Ombudsman has the mandate to identify patterns, trends, and systemic issues that contribute to administrative injustices. By addressing these underlying issues, the Ombudsman aims to prevent future grievances and enhance the overall functioning of institutions.

7) **Recommendations for Legal Action:**

In cases where the Ombudsman uncovers evidence of wrongdoing or violations of the law, they may recommend legal action be taken against responsible individuals or entities. This ensures that serious offenses are properly addressed through appropriate legal channels.

8) **Promotion of Fairness and Equity:**

The Ombudsman promotes fairness and equity in administrative decisions by examining whether policies and practices discriminate against certain groups or individuals. This function helps ensure that administrative actions do not unjustly disadvantage any segment of the population.

9) **Awareness and Education:**

Ombudsmen often engage in outreach and educational activities to raise awareness about individuals' rights, the role of the Ombudsman, and how to seek redress for grievances. Educating the public helps empower citizens to navigate bureaucratic processes effectively.

10) Reports to Authorities:

The Ombudsman may submit reports of their investigations, findings, and recommendations to relevant authorities, government bodies, or legislative bodies. These reports provide valuable insights for policymakers and lawmakers to improve administrative systems and address systemic issues.

4.4 Lokpal:

The concept of the Lokpal gained prominence in India as a result of widespread public demand for stronger mechanisms to combat corruption and hold public officials accountable. The Lokpal Act was passed by the Indian Parliament in 2013, and the Lokpal was established as an independent body to investigate and prosecute cases of corruption involving high-level officials. The Lokpal is empowered to inquire into allegations of corruption and misconduct, conduct investigations, and recommend action, including prosecution, against those found guilty of corrupt practices. It operates independently of the executive branch of government and is meant to act as a check on abuses of power.

4.4.1 Meaning of Lokpal:

"Lokpal" is a term derived from two Hindi words: "lok," which means "people," and "pal," which means "caretaker" or "protector." In the context of governance and public administration in India, "Lokpal" refers to an independent ombudsman institution established to investigate and address complaints of corruption against public officials and elected representatives at the central government level.

The Lokpal is designed to serve as a watchdog and guardian of integrity in the public sector. Its main function is to receive complaints from citizens about corruption or unethical conduct by public servants and elected officials, and to conduct thorough investigations into these allegations. The Lokpal aims to ensure transparency, accountability, and fairness in the functioning of government institutions.

4.4.2 Jurisdiction of Lokpal:

The Lokpal and Lokayukts Act, 2013 outlines the jurisdiction and powers of the Lokpal in India. Here's a general overview of the jurisdiction of Lokpal as per the Act:

1) **Central Government Employees:**

   The Lokpal has jurisdiction over central government employees, including officers and employees of corporations, authorities, boards, companies, societies, trusts, or autonomous bodies that are owned or controlled by the central government.

2) **Prime Minister:**

The Lokpal has the authority to receive complaints of corruption against the Prime Minister of India, except in matters related to national security, public order, atomic energy, space, and international relations.

3) **Union Ministers:**

The Lokpal can investigate allegations of corruption against Union Ministers.

4) **Members of Parliament:**

The Lokpal can investigate complaints of corruption against Members of Parliament.

5) **Group A and Group B Officers:**

The Lokpal can receive complaints of corruption against officers of Group A and Group B, as well as equivalent ranks, in central government departments and organizations.

6) **Public Functionaries:**

The Lokpal has jurisdiction over public functionaries who are not covered by the Central Government employees category, including those appointed by any statutory or constitutional authority.

7) **Investigation Agencies:**

The Lokpal can investigate allegations of corruption against officers of the Delhi Special Police Establishment (CBI) and officers of other investigation agencies that are notified by the central government.

It's important to note that the Act also provides for the establishment of Lokayuktas in states. Lokayuktas have similar jurisdiction at the state level as the Lokpal does at the central level. However, the jurisdiction of Lokayuktas may vary from state to state based on the specific legislation enacted by each state government.

4.4.3 Power and Functions of Lokpal:

Here's an overview of the key powers and functions of the Lokpal:

1) **Investigation of Complaints:**

The Lokpal has the power to inquire into allegations of corruption against public servants covered under its jurisdiction. It can initiate investigations based on complaints received from individuals or on its own accord.

2) **Search and Seizure:**

The Lokpal has the authority to conduct searches and seizures in cases related to corruption, subject to certain conditions and procedural safeguards.

3) **Prosecution:**

The Lokpal can initiate prosecution proceedings in special courts against individuals accused of corruption, based on the evidence collected during investigations.

4) **Recommendations for Action:**
   Upon completion of investigations, the Lokpal can recommend disciplinary actions, including penalties and sanctions, against public servants found guilty of corruption.

5) **Recommendations for Prosecution:**
   If the Lokpal finds sufficient evidence of corruption, it can recommend the initiation of criminal prosecution against the accused individuals.

6) **Monitoring of Investigations:**
   The Lokpal can monitor the progress of investigations and prosecution in cases it is handling, ensuring that the process is carried out effectively and in a timely manner.

7) **Whistleblower Protection:**
   The Lokpal has the power to provide protection to whistleblowers who report instances of corruption or misuse of power.

8) **Asset Declaration:**
   The Lokpal can require public servants to declare their assets and liabilities, which helps in preventing and detecting cases of disproportionate assets.

9) **Recommendations for Systemic Improvements:**
   Apart from investigating individual cases, the Lokpal can make recommendations for systemic improvements in the processes and procedures to prevent corruption.

10) **Public Awareness and Education:**
    The Lokpal can undertake activities to promote public awareness about corruption and its detrimental effects on society. It can also educate the public about their rights and responsibilities in reporting corruption.

11) **Advisory Role:**
    The Lokpal can provide advice to public authorities and organizations on measures to improve transparency, accountability, and integrity in their operations.

12) **Coordination:**
    The Lokpal can coordinate with various government agencies, departments, and institutions to ensure effective implementation of its decisions and recommendations.

4.5 Lok Ayukta:

The Lokayukta (also Lok Ayukta) is an anti-corruption ombudsman organization in the Indian states. Once appointed, Lokayukta cannot be dismissed nor transferred by the government, and can only be removed by passing an impeachment motion by the state assembly. Naresh Kadyan moved public interest litigation before High Court and then contempt of court order petition for not appointing Lokayukta in Haryana. The Administrative Reforms Commission (ARC) headed by Morarji Desai submitted a special interim report on "Problems of Redressal of Citizen's Grievances" in 1966. In this report, the ARC recommended the setting up of two special authorities designated as 'Lokpal' and 'Lokayukta' for the redressal of citizens' grievances.

The Lokayukta, along with the Income Tax Department and the Anti Corruption Bureau, mainly helps people publicise corruption among the Politicians and Government Officials. Many acts of the LokAyukta have resulted in criminal or other consequences for those charged.

Maharashtra was the first state to introduce the institution of Lokayukta through *The Lokayukta and Upa-Lokayuktas Act in 1971*. This was followed by similar acts that were enacted by the states of Odisha, Rajasthan, Bihar, Uttar Pradesh, Karnataka, Madhya Pradesh, Andhra Pradesh, Gujarat, Kerala, Tamil Nadu and the union territory of Delhi. The Maharashtra Lokayukta is considered the weakest Lokayukta due to lack of powers, staff, funds and an independent investigating agency. On the other hand, the Karnataka Lokayukta is considered the most powerful Lokayukta in the country.

4.5.1 Meaning of Lokayukta:

"Lokayukta" is a term used in India to refer to an anti-corruption ombudsman institution at the state level. The term "Lokayukta" is derived from Sanskrit, where "Loka" means people and "Yukta" means appointed or designated. In essence, a Lokayukta is an institution that represents the interests of the people by addressing complaints of corruption and maladministration by public officials within a particular state. The Lokayukta is designed to function as an independent body that investigates allegations of corruption and misuse of power by public servants in the state government and other local administrative bodies. It aims to ensure transparency, accountability, and integrity in the functioning of the government and its various departments.

4.5.2 Nature of Lokayukta:

The first Administrative Reforms Commission headed by Mr. Morarjee Desai recommended for Sweden based Ombudsmen type of institution. Accordingly the center can have Lokpal and states can have Lokayukta. Though the institution of Lokayukta was introduced for the first time in Odisha but it was not able to implement it. Maharashtra was the first state to implement in 1973. It investigates the allegation against officials like corruption, favouratism, nepotism, injustice and other grievances. It does not include Judges, Speaker, Chairman, Accountant General, Chairman and Members of State Public Service Commission, Judges of Civil and criminal court. The Lokayukta receives the petition from the public and conducts inquiries. It has power to raid on the houses and offices of corrupt official.

1) Lokayukta are appointed for 5 years or till attaining age of 70 years.

2) His salary is equivalent to Chief Justice of India and salary of its members is equivalent to Judge of Supreme Court.
3) They can be removed from the office by the governor, on the charge of misbehaviour or incapacity proved in the state legislature by 2/3rd majority.

4.5.3 Power and Functions of Lokayuktas:

Here's an overview of the typical powers and functions of Lokayuktas:

1) **Investigation of Complaints:**

   Lokayuktas have the power to investigate allegations of corruption, maladministration, and abuse of power by public officials within their respective states. They can initiate investigations based on complaints received from individuals or suo-motu (on their own accord).

2) **Search and Seizure:**

   Lokayuktas have the authority to conduct searches and seizures related to corruption cases, subject to legal requirements and procedural safeguards.

3) **Prosecution:**

   Lokayuktas can initiate prosecution proceedings against individuals accused of corruption and recommend appropriate legal action based on the evidence collected during investigations.

4) **Recommendations for Action:**

   After investigating a case, Lokayuktas can recommend disciplinary actions, penalties, or sanctions against public servants found guilty of corruption or maladministration.

5) **Recommendations for Prosecution:**

   If sufficient evidence is found, Lokayuktas can recommend the initiation of criminal prosecution against individuals involved in corrupt practices.

6) **Whistleblower Protection:**

   Lokayuktas can provide protection to whistleblowers who report instances of corruption or misconduct.

7) **Asset Declaration:**

   Similar to the Lokpal, Lokayuktas can require public servants to declare their assets and liabilities to prevent disproportionate assets accumulation.

8) **Systemic Reforms:**

   Lokayuktas can suggest systemic reforms and improvements in the functioning of government departments and agencies to prevent corruption and enhance transparency.

9) **Public Awareness and Education:**
Lokayuktas may engage in activities to raise public awareness about corruption and promote ethical governance. They can educate the public about their rights and responsibilities in combating corruption.

10) **Advisory Role:**
Lokayuktas can provide advice to public authorities and institutions on measures to enhance transparency, accountability, and integrity in their operations.

11) **Coordination:**
Lokayuktas can collaborate with various government bodies, departments, and organizations to ensure the effective implementation of their decisions and recommendations.

12) **Monitoring and Review:**
Lokayuktas can monitor the progress of investigations, recommend actions, and oversee compliance with their recommendations.

Review Questions

Q.1. Write Long Answers :

1) What is Good Governance? Explain the Characteristics of Good Governance.
2) Explain the Importance of Good Governance.
3) What is Corruption? Explain the Causes and Impacts of Corruption.
4) Discuss the Measures for Prevention to Corruption.
5) What is Ombudsman? State the Functions of Ombudsman.
6) Discuss in detail about the "Lokpal."
7) Explain the Meaning and Power of "Lokayukta."

Q.2. Short Notes :

1) Good Governance.
2) Administrative Corruption.
3) Ombudsman.
4) Lokpal.
5) Lokayukta.